PRAISE FOR FOOLISH

"FOOLISH puts a magnifying glass to the issues that have driven clients like me and advisors like Gil out of the brokerage world. Investors who are truly focused on the long term would be wise to follow the path Gil lays out. His perspective, especially when applied to investment strategy over a lifetime, is sure to not only reduce heartache and frustration but also generate superior returns."

—MIKE WALEN, FORMER COO, CABOT OIL AND GAS

"This priceless assembly of observations and remedies will save you years of agony and disappointment with your investments. Read this and follow this playbook."

—DUDLEY OLDHAM, RETIRED SENIOR
PARTNER, FULBRIGHT & JAWORSKI LLP

"The range of outcomes from activities involving risk is much wider than anyone wants to admit, and the results can be significantly better and significantly worse than we

want to believe. But throughout my years as an investor, I have come to believe that our performance in the midst of risk is the result of our actions and behaviors in the bad times as opposed to the good times. That's what this book hit home for me. The ideas reiterated, again and again, show that consistency and a commonsense approach to investing are what will position investors to succeed."

—RANDY LIMBACHER, FORMER COO,
BURLINGTON RESOURCES

"Life teaches us that 'due diligence' is necessary in all that we do. Regarding responsible investing, FOOLISH has done the due diligence for you."

—MIKE CALVERT, PRESIDENT, MIKE CALVERT TOYOTA

"FOOLISH tells it like it is. I've tried managing my money myself, I've tried enlisting brokerage firms to help, and I've tried to manage my money myself once again. I had neither the time nor expertise to devote to doing so. My journey has culminated in identifying someone whom I trust, who embraces the concepts outlined in this text, and who has the knowledge and expertise to execute a plan consistent with my vision."

—HUSSEIN ELKOUSY, MD

"I am blessed to represent some of the country's best investment managers. Very few firms have amassed, and continue to manage, assets as efficiently as Segment."

—THOMAS D. GIACHETTI, ESQUIRE,
CHAIRMAN, STARK & STARK

FOOLISH

FOOLI$H

HOW INVESTORS GET WORKED UP AND WORKED OVER BY THE SYSTEM

GIL BAUMGARTEN

LIONCREST
PUBLISHING

FOOLISH

How Investors Get Worked Up and Worked Over by the System

ISBN   978-1-5445-2000-1 *Hardcover*
      978-1-5445-1999-9 *Paperback*
      978-1-5445-1998-2 *Ebook*

I want to dedicate this book to Jack Bogle, who unfortunately died before it was complete. Jack was the father of the passive investing methodology and was relentless in his pursuit of strategies that benefit the client. He founded Vanguard in 1974 and introduced the first index fund at the end of 1975. Like me, he got crosswise with former employers who did not want his irrefutable methodology to prosper and who created roadblocks to ensure its death. Jack's understanding of, and willingness to share, the ways markets and portfolios actually function were critical to my understanding of how things should be positioned. My firm is equally relentless in our pursuit of what is best for our clients.

I also want to dedicate this book to my lovely wife, Sue, who has always been more confident in my abilities than I. She is just the best.

CONTENTS

DISCLAIMER

Before we dive in, I want to mention that I worked in the brokerage industry from 1985 to 2010. The opinions and personal experiences I discuss in this book are mine and are based on the modes and rules of operation I experienced in that time frame. We know costs have been dropping for many years, but due to the intentional opaqueness of brokerage firm operations, I cannot confirm that all the practices I have outlined are still in place. I can, however, say that I have done my best to reflect current information on costs and performance as of late 2020. The brokerage business is ever evolving, and recent legislation (Regulation Best Interest) has passed with the intention of forcing brokerage firms to mend some of their ways. How that manifests in true behavioral change is still unknown. I have no reason to believe there has been much change since the firms are so profitable and since the hotly debated landmark regulatory reform mentioned above still landed on the side of disclosure over behavioral change. Since so much money is at stake, these practices will only change with greater regulatory pressure that lobbyists are unable to defeat.

INTRODUCTION

THE JOURNEY AHEAD

The investment business is built on many misconceptions. Have you ever heard someone tell you they've made it? That they've found the perfect recipe for financial success? The truth is, everyone (including you) *wants* to beat the system, find the silver bullet, and uncover the secret of the ages. It just so happens there are major disadvantages to running down those trails.

Let's set a precedent for honesty right now: this book is *not a* "Get Rich 101." This book was primarily written for people who already have money, already have investing experience, and already have experienced investment disappointments. If you're looking for a book on getting rich quick, you might want to shut this one and put it back on your shelf. I'm not your guide to that end. But if you're hoping to walk through an honest door into the investment world, to better understand how to control your own financial future, this book *is* for you.

Individuals often spend loads of time, money, and mental energy crafting plans to invest and manage their wealth. As they begin to invest, however, they quickly realize how complicated and difficult the financial ecosystem is to navigate. Eventually, most seek a relationship with a broker or two or a trustworthy fiduciary advisor, who will advocate for them. Of course, they expect exceptional returns from their financial relationships, but in the end, they simply want relief. They don't want their financial well-being to be their problem anymore. They just want to be told what to do.

And here you are, having just opened this book, hoping to be relieved of something yourself. After all, who really wants to spend countless hours, hard-earned dollars, and mental toil thinking about what you have and have not, what you know and do not know, what you did and did not do, all while watching the market's volatile line move up and down? Why not hire a professional who can provide exceptional performance and peace of mind? It makes sense. And you may have done that a time or two—handed off the keys to your financial future. But then, things get trickier. Hiring the typical "professional" makes you vulnerable to "broker speak"—language that pledges to fulfill every investor's greatest hopes and aspirations through questionable investment schemes. These appeal to the driving forces of fear and greed, yet too often fail to deliver the gains they promise.

Is the problem the market? Is it the brokers, the advisors, the entire system?

We'll unpack these questions, the misconceptions, and the incomplete narratives later in the book, but here's the big picture: the problem is not just the system. The problem lies in *how* and *why* you make the investment decisions you do, including *who* your brokers and advisors are, *which* narratives you buy into, *when* you make your moves, and *what* choices you make. Trust me, you can do a whole lot better with a little nudge in the right direction.

No one book can answer all questions about individual predispositions and circumstances, but what you will find in the following pages is the culmination of 35 years of making my way through the investment business and pocketing my observations along the way. I don't claim to have everything figured out, but this is my take on where the industry has it right and where we all need to pay attention.

This book will take you on an honest journey to explore

not only the world of investing but also *yourself.* I'll be your guide. Buckle up.

TERMS TO KNOW

- **Financial Advisor:** Any financial service provider who can legally give financial advice. Stockbrokers, fiduciary advisors, and many others are all known professionally as financial advisors or simply "advisors," even though their individual roles vary greatly. This naming often confuses the general public.

- **Stockbroker (Broker):** A brokerage firm representative who is registered with the Financial Industry Regulatory Authority (FINRA) and who represents the firm in interactions with clients. The firm sets the rules on what and how investments are presented to clients within the regulatory framework established and monitored by FINRA. The firm also dictates the commissions charged and fees levied against client accounts and the split arrangement between the firm and its brokers. The firm occasionally modifies its split arrangements to incentivize the behavior it prefers from its broker representatives. Brokers cannot be fiduciaries but can offer fiduciary services provided by others, such as an advisory firm's separately managed account (SMA) services, also known as a wrap account.

- **Fiduciary Advisor:** One who is legally bound to limit or vanquish conflicts of interest in advising and dealing with clients and their investments but who cannot earn a commission on trades. A fiduciary advisor is paid for their advice, not for executing the trades themselves. In theory, this separation encourages the fiduciary advisor to always give the best financial advice to their clients whether or not that advice encourages a trade. (Meanwhile, a broker is incentivized to execute trades because that is how *they* receive compensation.) Fiduciary advisors must be registered with the Securities and Exchange Commission (SEC) as a registered investment advisor (RIA).

- **Brokerage Firm:** A FINRA-regulated firm that facilitates the buying and selling of financial instruments for a commission, shared fees, soft dollars, etc., and is offered wide latitude for conflicts of interest with clients.

- **Investment Manager/Money Manager:** An advisor for hire who makes investment decisions for investors through mutual funds or SMA services, which are based on a particular strategy and are not customized for each individual investor. These managers may work as a part of a brokerage firm or be independent and are usually registered with the SEC as an RIA. These managers almost never collect a commission for their services but instead charge a fee that is calculated as a percentage of assets under management (AUM).

CHAPTER ONE

THE HOUSE ALWAYS WINS

"Lesson number one: Don't underestimate the other guy's greed."

—*SCARFACE* (1983)

I haven't spent much time in casinos, but I know one thing for sure: the house always wins. Casinos are designed to influence human psychology and lower defenses. The lights, the colors, the free drinks, the glamour and allure of success—it all gets people to act in certain ways so that the house always wins. So it is with Wall Street. Wall Street always wins.

Even though Wall Street is a real place, "Wall Street" also refers to the entire financial services industry in the United States. So let me clarify: when I say "the house" I'm referring to the major brokerage firms, such as Merrill

Lynch, UBS, Morgan Stanley, and so forth. They're bent on winning, utilizing an ecosystem designed to take advantage of investor impulses, anxieties, and predispositions. Exploiting the emotions accompanying the unknowns and what-ifs, brokerage firms present themselves as the accommodating guides to the complex financial terrain. It just so happens they've designed much of that complexity themselves. The fancy suits, the exciting products, the pitches about excess returns—it all gets investors riled up to play "the game." The problem is that the game comes at great cost to the average individual investor, and it often fails to deliver the promised results.

If you have money to invest, you probably know what I'm talking about. Being successful sounds the alarm for commissionable opportunity, as people calling themselves "advisors" stand ready to give you their best pitch on why you should participate in their money-making brilliance.

Many of these advisors (who are technically brokers if they work for a brokerage firm) claim they can unlock the power of Wall Street on your behalf, which is fair, considering how often investors do poorly when they embark on their own. But the system is designed to benefit those firms more than it is to benefit you, the individual investor. Since these firms have interests that compete with those of their clients', they often don't counsel you on the best paths given your goals. Instead, they counsel on the best paths given *their* goals.

Don't worry. I'm not about to call out the suits on Wall Street for being a bunch of crooks. They're not. If we're calling anything crooked here, it would be the system, not the brokers. Every business has bad apples, but the vast majority of people in the financial business are moral and ethical. The problem is, although they are free to act morally and ethically, they're given bumpers for their lanes. Those bumpers force the balls to hit the pins one way or another, meaning every transaction must be profitable for the brokerage firm. Period.

It hasn't always been this way. In college, while studying economics, I vividly remember my impression of Wall Street as genteel, with country clubs and mint juleps. It seemed brokers knew their clients, their families, and their dreams and aspirations for their legacies. It sounded to me like a great place to earn a serious living and help people. That's why I joined.

I just didn't know that being behind Wall Street's closed doors would expose a new side of the business just a few short years after college.

WHAT'S IN IT FOR ME?

People tend to demonize and caricature Wall Street. I won't do that. After all, I worked for some of these brokerage firms. However, what I experienced as a broker was a firm culture that was entirely focused on what was best for itself. All that does is inspire greed, stimulate fear, and lead to frustration for both brokers and clients.

Allow me to explain.

The relationship between a brokerage firm and broker can be an easy one, as long as the broker is willing to put the firm's interest first. Brokerage firms incentivize their brokers to engage in activity profitable for the firm by making it profitable for the broker as well. For instance, is the broker considering selling a mutual fund to a client? They'll be sure to choose one that includes a 12b-1 fee (a hidden kickback) to ensure it's profitable for themselves. Are they pitching a client a hot stock? That'll bring in a trading commission which is split between the firm and the broker. Regardless of the transaction, the firm's message to the broker is the same: "Do what's profitable for us, and it will be profitable for you."

In broker vernacular, they must constantly be thinking of one question: *What's the YTB (yield to broker) on this?*

Here's my question: Did anyone stop to think about whether a path is optimal for the client?

From 35 years of experience, I can assure you the answer is far from satisfactory. Maybe the client was considered for a moment, but when the gears are built to propel in one direction (the brokerage firm's best interest), any contaminant just gums up the works. In the current system, there is no mechanism to ensure client benefit, only external regulations to ensure an investment is not "wrong" for the client (i.e., in outright opposition to the client's goals). Because of the mentality of brokerage firms and their sticky relationship with brokers, you ought to be skeptical of each idea they present to you.

Yes, businesses should aim to succeed. Every business should not only be thinking about your needs and how they can meet them but also about how they can play the right tune to get you to click "Buy It Now!" For most products or services, there's no harm in that strategy. We're all familiar with paying a markup on a product or service, and we purchase accordingly. But in most industries, there is either transparency or a multitude of options, so consumers get to decide if the price is right from a more informed position. Not so in the financial services industry, where complex cost structures and hidden fees shroud the client's understanding.

Further, although no business should provide a service without a compensation model, consumers ought to know exactly what they're paying for. If another company offers a similar service but gives the client better odds of ending up with more money in *their* pockets, instead of the pockets of the house, so to speak, consumers should know about that, too.

It's much more complicated in the financial services world because you're not buying just one product or subscribing to a monthly service, nor are you taking a quick weekend trip to Las Vegas where you know you're going to spend money on "playing the stakes." With financial advisors, you're purchasing access to professional relationships. They even toss around the term *advocacy*, telling you that they are your friend who's looking out for you. So, many trusting investors go in without knowing what they're getting themselves into, without knowing what the markups will be or where they will be coming from. Frankly, it's a bit of a convoluted mess.

In the middle of all this, there's you, the client, the individual investor. You have needs; the brokers have knowledge and access to solutions. One thing is for sure: you know that they know the markets better than you do, and you know they said they'd look out for you. All you can do is hope they hold up their end of the bargain.

The win-lose proposition of a casino is not identical to the Wall Street scenario, where it *is* possible for you and the service provider to both win simultaneously. Actually, the odds of winning are quite high for those who invest correctly. But the ecosystem at traditional brokerage firms siphons off profits for the firm, detracting from the investor's odds of success, and the firm wins regardless because the house always wins.

WELCOME TO THE SLAUGHTERHOUSE

I remember being on a road trip with my family when I was around 12 years old. We were all getting hungry, but we were in the middle of nowhere. Eventually, we came across this stand-alone taqueria, and my brother and I begged my mom to pull over. We walked in, and it felt like an oasis. It smelled amazing. I ran to the bathroom, and on my way out, I saw these cardboard boxes in the hallway that said, "Ground Beef. U.S. Canner." I walked back out to the table, wondering what that meant. When my mom explained that canner beef is the cheap stuff, one notch above dog food, I wondered what happened to my appetite. You'll never see a restaurant promote the fact that they use canned meat. That's because some things in life simply shouldn't be for sale.

Let's take a look at the case of Facebook "mishandling" users' personal information in 2018. The world's most dominant social media platform cut sharing deals with technology companies and other large businesses looking to purchase access to user data. The Federal Trade

Commission (FTC) went up in arms, and Facebook had to endure a record-setting fine to settle the matter. As you know, the FTC is an agency whose primary concern is to protect consumers, to advocate against fraud, deception, and unfair business practices. The moment a consumer's privacy is on the line, the FTC is trusted to step in and make things right. Right? In this case, at least, they did just that.

In the brokerage business, certain things should not be for sale, namely the relationship between the broker and the client. But that is precisely what gets sliced up and monetized by the brokerage firms, even while they use the term *advisor* when referring to their brokers. Considering that trust is the ultimate measure of success in a relationship, it's amazing what the brokerage firms are willing to sell that compromises that trust. The term *advisor* implies a sense of courtesy, comradery, and advocacy, don't you think?

So who's looking out for the client in all this? Well, the Securities and Exchange Commission (SEC). The SEC is responsible for protecting investors. Its job is not to ensure profitability but to make sure investors are not getting ripped off or defrauded. When individual investors are in harm's way, the SEC is trusted to step in and make things right. Right? And yet, ideas on how best to do that have changed over time, as the regulations reflect.

As I said, things used to be different.

A BRIEF HISTORY

Prior to the Great Depression, the stock market experienced unprecedented gains. So much so that even the banks wanted in on the action. Banks used their customer deposits to invest in the market, more speculatively than wisely, and participated in investment banking operations (such as initial public offerings and mergers and acquisitions). The sudden downturn in the stock market was devastating for banks, which at that time couldn't allow customer withdrawals. The downfall of the banks wiped out the savings of the population and led to years of suffering for the American people. In the aftermath, Congress enacted the Glass-Steagall Act, which mandated the separation of commercial banking (checking and savings accounts, consumer loans) from investment banking, requiring banks to follow strict safety protocols with their holdings.

The following years established a fresh reputation for banking: banks were again highly regarded and highly regulated and for many years largely unchanged. Banks existed to provide families and businesses an opportunity to earn a steady return in their savings accounts and to take out loans for their borrowing needs. As the economic policy of the '70s and '80s saw wild fluctuation in inflation and interest rates, investing in the stock market became increasingly popular. So much so, a sense of competition between banks and brokerage firms arose, and as a result, the banks were motivated to come up with new products and new ways of doing things.

What was the solution? Ultimately, banks, brokerage firms, and insurance companies (the three prongs of financial services) started buying each other or merging.

In 1998, Smith Barney, Travelers Insurance, and Citicorp announced a merger into Citigroup. At the time, this move violated the Glass-Steagall Act since this would again allow the threat of banks becoming "too big to fail" (when banks become so large and interconnected that their failure would be too catastrophic to allow). Yet, Congress had conveniently softened up to the idea of allowing bigger financial firms to merge in mega-industry conglomerates and the time was ripe for repeal. The Glass-Steagall Act was replaced with the passage of the Gramm-Leach-Bliley Act, partially laying the groundwork for the financial crisis of 2008.

I worked for Smith Barney at the time, one of the three of this new unholy trinity, who heralded this merger as a brave new step forward. I sat in the front row of the conference room in Houston that fateful day in 1998 when the Chairman of Smith Barney, Sanford "Sandy" Weill, gathered the troops for the big announcement. He extolled the virtues of the merger with Travelers Insurance and Citicorp, celebrating the opportunities before us in the virtually endless bounds that "cross-selling" now afforded.

I leaned over to my friend and fellow broker, Michael Brunner, and whispered, "This won't end well." He agreed. We were worried this reversion in regulation would lead us to the gates of something reminiscent of what happened in 1929. And sure enough, that's what happened in 2008. The reason was simple: as Winston Churchill said, "Those who fail to learn from history are condemned to repeat it."

Sure, the merger brought about synergies. Imagine how profitable it would be for brokerage firms and insurance companies to gain access to already-developed client relationships, and vice versa. A preexisting relationship comes with intel about which customers have money and what their needs are. Not to mention, all these services residing under one roof meant products would be cheaper for the companies to provide (but not cheaper for the customers!). You can see why Sandy Weill had sugar plums dancing in his head.

For big banks with oodles of FDIC-insured and leveraged cash, it now paid to swing hard. They set up performance bonus pools, essentially setting the dogs loose to sniff out extra profits. They also tried to mass produce their client relationships and maximize the value in between those lines, and they sure weren't wanting to let anything fall through the cracks.

Remember, in 2016, when Wells Fargo opened millions of new accounts for clients who didn't ask for them, resulting in fines of $185 million and the termination of 5,300 employees? In 2017, that same company was fined a cool $386 million for requiring 570,000 clients to purchase unnecessary insurance on their auto loans. They also caused deliberate delays in processing payments and then charged clients for missing deadlines on mortgages. Yeah, you can thank the bonus pool for all those little bundles of joy. The banks incentivized this bad behavior within their ranks but wanted employees to have the moral clarity to know where the nonsense should stop.

It sounds a bit like a slaughterhouse to me. At a slaughterhouse, there are systems designed to capture every little thing that could be usable after parts for human consumption are taken out. You name it, they use it. Skin trimmings, hair, bones, and hooves are made into products for animal feed. Fat is rendered into tallow, which is used as a lubricant in steel rolling and is oftentimes an ingredient in makeup and soap. Blood? Yep, that's in fertilizer. Feathers? You might find them in dog food and farm feed, too. The slaughterhouse makes money on the scraps, and frankly, they have a natural responsibility to do so.

The thing is, the people running the slaughterhouse never said they represented the interests of the animal. Not so on Wall Street. On Wall Street, your broker uses terms like *wealth management*, or *advisor*, or *practically fiduciary*, which leads you to expect a certain amount of allegiance.

Additionally, they have an incentive to maximize the embedded costs in the system, especially when they own all the layers of that system. Do you think they will refer you to a low-cost insurance policy when they own the one with higher costs and "better" commissions? Unless they're registered as a "fiduciary," they have no legal obligation to do so, and they won't. Imagine if the IRS paid your CPA a percentage of the total tax bill they calculated for you. How much would you trust your accountant?

Your relationship with your "advisor" shouldn't be monetized the same way as Beefmaster cattle. Yet it is.

Wall Street brokerage firms will sell layers of client relationships in the open market for profit. Here are a few "inedible" examples.

SCRAP #1: WALL STREET SELLS ACCESS TO THEIR BROKERS.

Brokerage firms know that the influence their brokers have over clients is valuable. And because mutual fund companies (and other marketing-centric financial product companies) are always looking for creative ways to sell their funds in bulk (and have a budget for it), brokerage firms put the shelf space in a broker's mind up for sale! They make room for pitchmen to stand in front of a room of brokers and extol the virtues of their funds, as long as they pay the fee and provide lunch. Brokerage firms are always thinking, "We have influence over the client. Who will pay for that?"

SCRAP #2: WALL STREET SWAPS SERVICES TO BENEFIT THE FIRM...AT CLIENT COST.

Wall Street brokerage firms have many lines of business that all need to turn a profit for the firm. They own entities such as mutual fund businesses, trading platforms, investment banking and corporate finance departments, and asset management businesses. A lot of "back scratching" goes on between these competing interests and swapping tit-for-tat is rampant. This drives client costs higher. You would think that this would eventually lead to a client exodus. But clients don't really know about the ways it affects them, and the business is "sticky," meaning it requires so much effort to pack up and move your assets that people tend to stick around, even when there are better options available.

SCRAP #3: WALL STREET CAPITALIZES ON CLIENT CAPTIVITY.

Brokerage firms know how sticky client-broker relationships are, so they make existing brokerage firm clients pay a premium for their "captivity." This is prevalent in the bond offerings at brokerage firms, municipal bonds in particular, because by nature, munis have a limited number of bonds per issuer. That makes them harder to compare and price check. When a broker shows a bond to a client, he prices it one way, and when I, an institutional buyer, buy the same bond, I'm shown a cheaper price on the exact same quantity. There are several reasons for this but none more important than the fact that I own software that tracks the live pricing of every single bond trade. Although I can quickly know precisely what that dealer paid for the bond, a brokerage client has no way to know and is not inclined to ask.

SCRAP #4: WALL STREET FACILITATES "MANAGED ACCOUNT" SERVICES WHERE PROFITS AND FEES GET STACKED.

I'll start by clarifying what I mean by "managed account."[1] Many clients open brokerage accounts and interact one-on-one with their brokers. The broker makes trade recommendations based on the client's stated goals. A "managed account," however, is a service that a broker/

---

[1] A managed account, also known as a wrap account, is an account service provided by brokerages where trading commissions and separate manager fees are waived in favor of an all-encompassing fee that pays the brokerage firm, the broker, and the manager in a split arrangement.

advisor often recommends to their client. It involves hiring a third-party investment manager who will direct trades in their account in accordance with a predefined strategy. Brokerage firms prefer this arrangement and incentivize their brokers to recommend it (considering the benefit to their brokerage firm's stock price since recurring revenue is more valuable than lumpy commissions).

When I was a broker at UBS, the client's stated cost of engaging an independent investment manager to run a managed account was 2.8 percent of the value of the account annually. Fees would decline from that point based on account size and negotiated fee rate. The firm was careful to word craft the fee-split arrangement with the broker because they saw an opportunity to make money sneakily. They would claim the cost to the firm of hiring the manager was 0.50 percent and deduct that from the client fees before the remainder hit the broker's "pay grid" (the spreadsheet that sorts out the broker's cut). For a client paying 2 percent annually, 1.5 percent would be the amount a broker was splitting with the firm 45/55 percent. I was curious how the math worked, so I dug around, asking questions of the managed account personnel, who reassured me that 0.50 percent was indeed what the independent investment manager was paid and that the brokerage firm did not profit by marking up the cost.

Five years later, I was an advisor at my fledgling registered investment advisor (RIA) firm. I happened to take a meeting with a woman who had worked at the managed account desk at another big-name brokerage firm. As we talked about our respective tenures at these firms, I saw my opportunity to find out the truth about the math of managed accounts. When I asked her how the firm profited from the managed account fee arrangement, she revealed that the firm *did* mark up the cost of the third-party managers! Surprise, surprise. She said that brokers were charged 0.50 percent of the client fee by the firm for the "managed account service," and the firm, in turn, paid the manager's firm a mere 0.25 percent or less. When I asked about all the cloak and dagger, she revealed that the brokerage firm held regular meetings with the managed account desk personnel to teach them how to obfuscate the truth from curious brokers like me who asked too many questions. They would even engage in role-play to learn how to essentially lie when answering these questions, because the firm feared a revolt if too many brokers were aware that they were getting double-dipped.

SCRAP #5: BROKERS ARE INCENTIVIZED TO CHOOSE CERTAIN MUTUAL FUNDS FOR CLIENTS.

Mutual fund sales are a preferred way to get paid on Wall Street because investors don't give the costs enough scrutiny. The true costs are somewhat hidden from investors because fees are not shown as a deduction on clients' statements; mutual fund fees are charged daily but are deducted before the value of the fund units are declared at day's end. Meanwhile, investors believe the services they're receiving must be "free" because they think costs cannot exist if they don't see them. The brokerage firms then comply with lax regulatory rules by publishing disclosure documents they know clients won't read.

In the disclosure documents (called a prospectus), investors see an "expense ratio," which is quoted as a percentage of invested assets and includes the costs of investment management, legal, accounting, auditing, and even "advertising and promotion." Yet the cost of advertising and promotion includes a kickback to the broker and the brokerage firm (known as a 12b-1). Clearly, the brokers are not motivated to choose share classes with lower fees, and many investors are under the impression that they don't have other options.

There are generally six or so versions, or share classes, of each mutual fund, all identical except in how costs and commissions are applied. These share classes are distinguished by the breakpoints that exist at certain dollar levels. Clients graduate to the next cheaper share class when the purchase amount reaches a new breakpoint (meaning smaller clients tend to get the most expensive share classes and the larger clients tend to get the cheapest versions). Unscrupulous brokers can deny access to the cheaper versions of the fund in deliberate schemes that involve dropping purchase tickets in a particular order to maximize client charges. Brokerage firms have had to become much more diligent about reducing incentives and increasing penalties for brokers who engage in commission-gouging activities such as maneuvering around breakpoint incentives. Still, this practice, coupled with a lack of supervision, has resulted in some large legal settlements affecting the majority of brokerage firms.

SCRAP #6: WALL STREET HAS NO PROBLEM TALKING OUT OF BOTH SIDES OF THEIR MOUTHS.

Many Wall Street brokerage firms provide investment banking services to corporate clients for huge fees while also providing investment customers with research on those same companies. This research often leads to trades for which trading commissions are charged. This glaring conflict of interest has led to situations in which analysts base their research opinions not on company fundamentals but on whether publishing a favorable opinion would win the firm more investment banking deals. Likely the most flagrant example occurred back in the technology heyday of the late 1990s. Jack Grubman of Solomon Smith Barney was simultaneously working as both a technology analyst and an investment banker, making over $20 million per year. Jack was permanently barred from the brokerage industry after it came to light that he was publicly offering favorable opinions of certain companies while privately criticizing them. His cozy relationship with Worldcom executives was exposed after his firm's $12 billion WCOM bond offering ended in bankruptcy after his zealous cheerleading. In a similar fiasco, he admitted to changing his opinion to "favorable" on AT&T in an attempt to garner favor with a board member of a school in which he hoped to enroll his twin daughters.

This is not an isolated case. Brokerage firms have been known to change their research opinions in return for investment banking deal flow and compensation across a broad spectrum of conflicted "opportunities."

SCRAP #7: WALL STREET BROKERAGE FIRMS HAVE A "PAY-TO-PLAY" MANAGER RESEARCH DATABASE.

When a broker advises a client to use a managed account, the broker often consults a database (provided by the brokerage firm) to evaluate their options. The database includes filters for things such as yield, historical returns, investment style (i.e., large-cap value), and historical volatility (a crude measure of risk). This is a useful tool to narrow down an abundance of options. And even though there are plenty of options, there's one aspect of the database that isn't mentioned—the fact that the managers pay to be included on the list in the first place. That's right, independent investment management firms pay a fee to brokerage firms to be included in those evaluations, and those who don't pay, can't play. One could argue that the firms were never seeking the best manager candidates, just the best among those willing to "share the love."

I'm guessing you've caught the whiff of the septic tank by now. But here comes the coup de grâce of egregious behavior.

SCRAP #8: WALL STREET SELLS GLIMPSES OF CLIENT TRADE ACTIVITY TO A THIRD PARTY PRIOR TO EXECUTION.

Wall Street allows a form of front running[2] on your trade. This practice has some benefits to clients, so don't have a cardiac arrest just yet. Rapid-fire traders pay for fractional-second glimpses of trading activity, allowing them to turn tiny profits by showing up just before you. Although this can open up a Pandora's box of conflicts of interest, it has some positive effects. Clients normally won't pay a higher cost on that trade than the bid or ask side. Front running simply inserts a middleman with advance knowledge of

---

2   Front running is an illegal practice whereby advance knowledge of client trades could create an exploitable opportunity to trade against the client. It is not illegal if the firm or broker merely sells the info to a third party, provided that the front running that occurs from such information operates within the existing bid-ask spread. There are two possible objectionable results: the stock may be run up or down in front of a buy or sell order and the broker may use their position for gain.

what's coming, allowing a risk-free trade and a slice of the bid-ask spread.[3]

I know what you're thinking: *Wait, my information is not a secret up until the point the trade is executed?*

It's a secret up to a fraction of a second before execution, then they show it to a paying third party, who gets to use an algorithm to run out in front of your trade with that information.

You mean, they would allow someone the advantage of knowing what I'm going to do so that they can profit from my trade coming down the pipeline and right before my burst of water emerges, they're standing there to catch the first drop?

Yep.

Is your jaw on the floor yet? You should have seen my shiny face turn grim as I watched these operations take place. But the thing is, it's all just part of the business of guaranteeing the house will win. The firms' profits come from clients doing business within one or more parts of the system. The mutual fund company whose market-

---

3   The bid-ask spread refers to the difference between the highest price a buyer will pay and the lowest price a seller will accept. Most investments such as stocks or bonds have one price if you're buying and another if you're selling. Many middlemen make their living in that spread and often have their own money at risk.

ers are paying for shelf space at the brokerage firm? The fund shareholders paid for that. What about the managed account client, when the manager is paying for "evaluations"? Those costs get passed along to clients ultimately. It's all a giant skimming operation and it's the clients (and occasionally the brokers) getting skimmed. And skimming is fine when it's known, but it is surely not fine when it's hidden and cloaked in words of advocacy.

The system has morphed into a giant, fee-extracting machine, and the brokerage firms are happy participants. I'll go ahead and drive this home for you.

I spent a decade working for a US brokerage firm owned by a huge Swiss bank with offices throughout Europe. One day, a longtime US client of mine called to say he and his wife were buying a house in Spain. They needed $900,000 in US dollars converted to euros and wired to a bank in Spain. They wanted to know if my company's Spanish division could help. Amazingly, my Swiss firm said they could do the conversion to euros for "free."

I asked for a description of "free."

They said, "No spreads, no markups,[4] client trades at

---

4   A markup refers to when a firm takes possession of an investment from a seller, client, or other brokerage firm with their own capital and increases the buyer's price, or decreases the seller's price, to earn a "spread." This is regulated as a commission.

spot."[5] For clarity, the term *spot* refers to the frictionless (devoid of any transaction costs) institutional price for any commodity at any moment in time. In disbelief and afraid I had misunderstood, I asked for a supervisor on the New York currency desk. She came on the line, and I repeated the prior conversation. She confirmed the description; zero cost to the client and "since the firm doesn't make a penny, there's no commission for you." I was fine with that since a "free" trade should have no commission. I conveyed this to the client who asked to move forward. The trade occurred and my client was charged $900,000 with zero commission to me. The euros were wired to the bank the client had specified. Then the client called and said he was missing about $2,700. The client had been watching the currency market trading live and had seen his $900,000 trade come across the ticker with the spot price listed. He did the math and said the price on his trade confirmation wasn't "spot" after all. I called the supervisor on the desk and started asking questions. I asked how I could have misunderstood her when she said, "Spot." She said, "Well, there's spot, and then there's *spot*." She went on to explain that the firm had a big European presence and could trade in its own account at spot overseas. They then marked those trades up about three-tenths of 1 percent and returned *that* price to the US market as "spot." I asked

---

5   Spot refers to the institutional live price in the marketplace at a moment in time for any
    commodity or currency which reflects large size and liquidity void of all commissions
    or markups.

her how that jibed with her previous comment that "the firm doesn't make a penny on this." She said, "I guess they do when you look at it like that." My head exploded.

Fortunately for me, the firm, and the client, I had a reasonable supervisor. He was not surprised by any of this, but he was equally horrified when I explained the turn of events. He knew that undoing what had been done was impossible thanks to the byzantine structure, now including a foreign currency trading desk. He simply had his error account drop $2,700 into my client's account. This underhanded transaction likely ended up costing that firm more than $25 million. That's because no single event in my prior 25 years as a broker did more to motivate me to leave the brokerage business and take my clients with me.

There are dozens of these examples I could share, but those above are the most egregious. I spent 25 years of my career working on Wall Street before I re-registered as a fee-only fiduciary advisor and gave up my broker's license. What I saw behind closed doors led me to branch off and start my own firm back in 2010, with a different type of registration and entirely different rules of engagement with clients. We'll get more into my story in the next chapter, but you need to know from the start that I'm an old-time insider calling BS on how these firms handle their client relationships. I have always cared about the individual investor first, and I want you to win, not the house. I hope that if I can transfer a little bit of knowledge about how this all works, you can turn many of the tables back to your advantage.

CLARIFYING CRUCIAL TERMS IN THIS BOOK

The titles, registrations, and designations found in the financial services world are confusing. Many call themselves "financial advisors," but that does not always mean what you might think. For the purposes of this book, we will use the term *financial advisor* generally to refer to all who offer financial advice but mainly brokers and fiduciary advisors. These are covered in more detail in Chapter 7.

Although brokerage firms allow some of their senior brokers to run accounts on a discretionary and fee-only basis (acting in a mostly fiduciary manner), that doesn't preclude them from earning commissions and serving in a nonfiduciary capacity in other accounts. This is facilitated in both the Portfolio Management (PM) and Guided Portfolio Management (GPM) programs at Smith Barney and the Portfolio Management Program (PMP) program at UBS. I built my practice on the discretionary side of the brokerage platform, which allowed me to run my business as close to fully fiduciary as possible. Nonetheless, all of the blockades discussed in this book are what led me to start my own fully fiduciary business.

CHAPTER TWO

WALL STREET, FRIEND OR FOE?

"There's no education like adversity."

—BENJAMIN DISRAELI, FORMER PRIME
MINISTER OF GREAT BRITAIN

When my kids were growing up, they were routinely asked what their dad did for a living. My boys would shrug and say, "Oh, something in finance?" but my daughter, Allie, being my most curious child, really tried to wrap her mind around how it all worked. One day, she asked me for a more in-depth explanation of my "something in finance" business. As I shared about portfolios and what my role in a client's decision-making process looked like, I grabbed the salt and pepper shakers from the table and said, "These two shakers represent the various ways I can help a client make money. The pepper shaker represents all the choices I can make that benefit me greatly and might also benefit the client. The saltshaker represents all the choices I can make that are more likely to benefit the client but are less likely to benefit me. I always choose the salt." When she asked why I would do that, I told her there was no doubt choosing the salt would benefit me, too, but in the long run.

ADVERSITY PAYS

When I have a rare moment of deep self-reflection and consider my journey as a man and as a businessman, I realize that at first glance there was little in my childhood that would have hinted at a life, a perspective, and a career path like mine.

My father practically raised himself on the streets of Galveston, Texas. He had no father figure, and his mother's attempts to teach and guide him on the straight and narrow were to no avail. He started smoking when he was fourteen, became a teenage petty criminal, and landed in military school as an alternative to jail. I like to say he was a bit "feral," but the reality is, he was simply not a good guy because he didn't know any better. He was pretty slick, though. He slithered his way in and out of money, convinced my mother to marry him, and eventually had two sons, me being the younger of the two.

I remember pleading with my dad to buy me a minibike

when I was about eight years old. When he reached his limit on my incessant pestering, he pulled out a yellow pad of paper and started scheming how he would design a rigged raffle to get the money to buy the minibike (which I would win). He never ended up doing anything with his grand plan, but the idea alone revealed how conniving he could be.

As I'm sure you can imagine, ours was a somewhat dysfunctional family. Between maneuvering with the IRS and pursuing other schemes to scratch his selfish itches, my dad had just enough time to leave my mom, brother, and me with the consequences of tax liabilities, loan defaults, and each our fair share of emotional baggage. My parents' marriage ended when I was 11 years old, and the day he walked out was the day I decided I would be nothing like him. Where he brought confusion, I wanted to bring clarity. Where he looked out for himself, I wanted to look out for my family and others. Where he sought short-term satisfaction, I wanted to build a life I could be proud of.

Of course, those achievements don't happen overnight. The mess my father made took time to wade through. His past cast a shadow on me, but I had to believe that he did not define me. His failures could only be fatal in my life if I let them be. I was determined to make it, to bring order to the lives around me. Over the years, a foundation of integrity, a determined self-sufficiency, and a strong work ethic set in, and I decided to work hard and keep busy. The adversity of my childhood would not have the last word.

My mom went on to do a great job raising my older brother and me, reversing much of the damage my father had wreaked. Miraculously, she was able to keep our household afloat despite her meager earnings as a nurse (and despite the fact that my award-winning father had taken all but $50 with him), allowing us to attend one of the best public high schools in Houston, Mirabeau B. Lamar.

My best friend all through high school at Lamar was a guy named Hugh Tullos. He had great parents, and his dad was a leading orthopedic surgeon in town. They lived a great life, with fancy cars and fancy trips, and I longed for a life like theirs. I never really felt jealous; I was merely an admirer who appreciated being invited in as a friend. The thing is, though, I was determined to someday have a great family and financial freedom like they did. And so, money was something I knew I had to figure out. I set out on an investigation and would always tell myself, "If it is to be, it's up to me."

I got my first job at the hospital where my mom worked as a nurse in the early 1970s. I made $1.75 an hour, and nothing felt as sweet as that cash in my hands at the end of the week. I worked hard and saved up to fund my entrepreneurial hobbies, including tinkering with cars, which

I enjoyed buying and trading. I always wanted to know how things worked and how I could make them work better. I appreciated the new experience of having a job, and becoming a consumer brought my attention to the various economic structures I encountered.

I think my curiosity can be attributed to my upbringing; there's something about growing up with nothing that will teach you how to jury-rig just about anything. I took things apart to figure out how to put them back together, sometimes breaking them in the process. One time, Hugh and I stumbled across a crashed motorcycle and turned it into a go-cart. If you asked either of us, we'd both say that was one of the greatest projects—turning junk into a new toy.

Around the time I graduated high school, my mom expressed to me how much she wished she were able to give us more. I shrugged that sentiment off because I had a feeling that if she had given us more, my life might be rather unsatisfying, void of the grind that I knew was shaping me into a better man. I went off to college, feeling fortunate to have grown up in an environment that taught me how to make something out of nothing. I simply had to figure out what to do with this knowledge to turn it into a career.

I considered becoming a doctor like Dr. Tullos, but chemistry did me in. Although engineering might have been my calling, I switched to the business school and could not figure out why the classes that seemed to come easily to me were the ones striking the most fear in my classmates. This natural bent soon evolved, and the more I learned about how money and investments worked, the more I leaned toward a career on Wall Street. So that's what I did. I later found it intriguing to uncover how similar my story was to those of other top advisors in the business.

My first job on Wall Street was at EF Hutton. After I spent four years building up my brokerage practice, the firm was bought out by Shearson Lehman. The new Shearson management immediately asked me to consider becoming a branch manager. It seemed like an interesting move, so I took the position. I soon determined that being a branch manager for a brokerage firm was absolutely the worst job on Wall Street. But during that two-year stint from '89 to '91, I learned massive amounts of information about the inner workings of the brokerage business, much of which I'm sharing here.

During my branch manager stint, one of the projects assigned to me was to call the brokerage firm's top 100 advisors and ask them a series of questions about their lives. We were looking for the commonalities in their stories. When I compiled the answers, I was stunned by the results. The single most significant predictor of a future top producer at the brokerage firm was family financial trauma as a teenager. This commonality seemed to produce the personal characteristic most vital to success: grit, otherwise known as resilience. Ask a top-producing broker about their life, and you will seldom hear that they come from wealth.

More often, you hear stories like that of the legendary super-broker Don Sanders, who was raised by his aunt and uncle in humble Mexia, Texas. He started sacking groceries at the age of 12 and later went on to have a wildly successful career in the financial services industry. His firm, Sanders Morris Harris, now has $11 billion in client assets under management (AUM).

So when my mother (who is 89 as I write this in 2020) goes on her routine spree of reminiscing about her successes and failures in life, her joys and regrets, she always mentions wishing she could have made my upbringing less traumatic. I tell her to be careful what she wishes for because things turned out just fine for me.

SWIMMING UPSTREAM

Yes, I was motivated by a desire to make a good living, but I also just like to figure out the best way to do things and help others do the same. And that's precisely what I set out to do when I got into the brokerage business back in

1984. As time went on, I began to notice my interests and my clients' interests were never fully aligned with those of the brokerage firms. I did my best to advocate for my clients, but the firm often opposed the best solution for the client, and boy, was that opposing current strong!

One of the most explicit pictures of this opposing current involves a conversation I had with a boss of mine. At the time, I had about 200 clients and I had plans to make a similar set of trades for many of them. The problem was that these trades were caked with complexities to allow middlemen a piece of the action at the clients' cost. There was a direct path possible, avoiding all the middlemen, but I knew the firm had set at least three roadblocks to prevent me from going that route. As I contemplated how I could make a way around these blockades, I ran into my boss in the long hallway between my office and his. I told him what I was trying to do and complained that my clients were disadvantaged because of these roadblocks created by the firm. He chuckled and said, "You know what your problem is? You think you work for the client! And that's just it; you work for the brokerage firm. The sooner you realize that, the less frustrating your life will be."

He laughed but was soon uncomfortable when he realized that I wasn't laughing. I could tell by the way he looked at me that he was serious about what he said but was more comfortable couching it in a chuckle. I suddenly realized

I had been going about this all wrong. I decided right then and there that he and I weren't even in the same business. I knew that if I was going to stay at the brokerage firm, I would have to toe the company line to be successful. That wasn't going to happen.

My boss either didn't see what I saw, or he did and simply didn't care. From what I knew of him, he was a great and moral guy trying to run a great and moral practice. But there was a way things had to be done, and everyone just went with the flow. Although the majority of brokers and financial advisors may believe they are doing what's best for the client, they are implanted in a business model that slices and dices the client relationship in ways that create conflicts of interest. As I've said, that's not an inherent problem as long as it's disclosed and acknowledged, but usually it is not.

The brokerage firm was primarily interested in making money, and if clients' needs were served along the way, then great. There was no intention to harm clients, but there was also no intention to choose the most beneficial path for the client, especially if it did not serve the brokerage firm. That's where the blockades came into play. Every time I made headway swimming upstream, the firm put up a new blockade to get me back in the flow. I believed that the current needed a change in direction. But just as river currents work, there's not much hope for a shift in the entire topography. My German DNA caused me to loathe the inefficiency. I began to feel like I was playing a giant pinball game. I tried to guide the steel ball through the maze without touching anything, but the firm's business depended on me pushing the ball into every bumper to ring the bells and flash the lights. And when I wouldn't cooperate, they would move the bumpers directly into my path. It was like a hellish funhouse.

My boss and I had more conversations about my desire to skim less by providing clients with more direct access. I explained that I was certain that direct access to markets using efficient vehicles such as exchange-traded funds (ETFs) would provide a better investment experience for clients. He and the firm resisted. I explained how ETFs work and why the costs and taxes are so much lower for clients. My boss tried to convince me that I was making a huge error by casting my lot with the clients because he was incentivized to keep me beholden to the firm. He said, "Good luck making a living at that." He was convinced clients would only buy into stories of sexy advantages, and the boring compounding stuff was for independent financial advisors who weren't in the brokerage business.

Precisely!

So I took the plunge. I started building low-cost, tax-efficient portfolios at the brokerage firm—each piece placed to maximize client benefit. And it worked well. I became increasingly intentional about building all of my clients' portfolios this way. I got rid of anything packaged by the firm, including mutual funds, unit trusts, and so forth.

I was very careful not to allow any proprietary tentacles of the firm to be found in my clients' accounts because I saw an opportunity to make an exit from the brokerage business and jump into a different flow entirely. The new topography would be designed to serve my clients' needs. I would let the chips fall where they may, whether it was profitable for my new firm or not. The client's good would be my duty, whereas beforehand, it was a distant second to following the brokerage firm's playbook. The cherry on top? It would all turn out to be quite profitable for my clients and for me.

BUILT TO LAST

Since I started my own firm in 2010, I have seen countless clients come through my office door, seeking a different kind of guide. My colleagues and I explain that ours is a tax-sensitive, fee-only fiduciary firm, meaning that we are required to serve clients' best interests and minimize conflicts of interest. Most potential clients don't even ask for proof of performance. For most, learning about the difference in methodology is more than enough for them to entrust me with their family legacies.

I remember one client named Mike, who was referred by his CPA. He came through my door, having had some super frustrating experiences with several brokerage firms. He decided to open an account with us and try doing things my way. Mike trusted us with his money, and we actually became friends outside of our partnership.

One day while Mike and I were on a hunting trip, I noticed that his former employer's stock (of which he held a large position) had jumped up by $8. We had discussed selling call options[6] against this position, and this stock price movement signaled it was time to get started. I told Mike it was go-time; that he could get $100,000 in option premium on 20,000 shares of stock. Mike gave the go-ahead, and I reached out to my team back at the office. Options trading requires special signed paperwork, which we had on file but not for the account number in which his stock resided. Our team got to work moving the shares electronically, but this caused a thirty-minute delay in getting his options sold.

That thirty minutes proved important because the stock weakened a bit, and the $100,000 option value I had quoted to Mike had faded to $95,000 by the time his order was executed. I told Mike what had happened, and he half-jokingly said, "Sounds like I got screwed out of

---

6   A call option is a financial instrument that gives the buyer an option to buy an asset (such as stocks) at an agreed-upon price on or before a particular date.

five grand over some paperwork snafu." I told him that I would research the details on time and price when I got back to the office, and if it turned out that time delay was, in fact, the culprit, I would make it right. As it turned out, he surely could have gotten a full $5,000 more if not for the delay, and the paperwork snafu was undeniably the problem. I reported it to him as such. He said in typical Texas twang, "Whatcha gonna do 'bout it?" I said, "I'm gonna give you the five grand I owe you." I could hear the wheels in his head turning in the silence on the other end of the phone. Here was a guy, a gen-u-wine muckety-muck retired C-suite executive, a board member of another public company, a man well versed in watching brokers wiggle out of responsibility. After a long pause and a deep sigh, he slowly said, "Here's what I'm gonna do...I'm gonna send you another $10 million to manage, 'cuz that's what we do with heads-up guys."

Wow!

My prior employer absolutely, positively would not have allowed me to fix this issue because it wasn't a true error; it was a clerical oversight. This situation would have required me to wiggle out of responsibility, as Mike surely expected because this kind of behavior may have been part of the less-than-satisfying experiences he had with brokers. At my new registered investment advisor (RIA) firm, this was a quick journal entry. I simply reversed $5,000 of his earlier fees paid, which I am free to do at any time, for any reason I deem appropriate. It took five minutes to fix, and he saw the money in his account before the end of the day.

As financial advisors and brokers, we play a particularly influential role in the client's life. People are complex, financial markets are complicated, and money management systems can be rigid. That's why our roles exist. Clients want an advocate who understands them and the system and can then use their knowledge of both to plan an optimal path forward. Since I've lived within the ecosystem that puts blockades in that optimal path, it sure is nice to swim freely and provide my clients with the advice and services they need to succeed.

CHAPTER THREE

———

THE WONDERS OF WALL STREET

"You can't expect a man to understand something which his job depends on him not understanding."

—WILL ROGERS, ACTOR, HUMORIST

Virtually all of us are connected to Wall Street in some fashion. Wall Street is chock-full of smart and honest people who want to do right by their clients. But, by design, every broker on Wall Street has a monkey on their back (the brokerage firm) who must be served first.

Most brokers would like to deliver the services that are truly best for you, but those services don't always pay the broker well. The brokers at the firm have a certain profitability mandate, and in order to meet it, they are incentivized to provide less-than-optimal solutions. You have to understand that the firm gets the bulk of the revenue, leaving the broker with only the residue. Thus, the broker is forced to hand you the most "mutually beneficial" services, so to speak. They might say they're looking out for you, but they always mean "within my limited choices," dictated by the firm. It just so happens that many of the firm's choices also tend to generate unnecessary taxes, which degrade client performance.

How is this allowed? The standard of care in the brokerage business hinges on the word *suitability*, dictated by FINRA Rule 2111, meaning the investment choice must not be inappropriate for the investor given their predisclosed risk tolerance and objectives. It also means that your broker is shielded from liability as long as they recommend "suitable" choices.

Most people simply aren't satisfied with "suitable." We want the best. We're nuts about quality, bang for the buck, and overall good experiences. Take my son Brian, for example. He absolutely loves the best of the best. He will dig through reviews for hours on end, call friends for reference, and do whatever it takes to make the best possible choice for everything. As you can imagine, when Brian needed a shoulder operation, he wasn't going to settle for "suitable." A doctor who offers "suitable" results only means he won't operate on the wrong arm. In the end, one of Houston's famed orthopedic surgeons, Dr. Hussein Elkousy, operated on Brian's shoulder, and within months he was back to participating in the activities he loves.

I don't like "suitable" either, and neither should you. Remember when AT&T rolled out a relatable suite of commercials likening cell service to other areas of life such as sushi, surgery, and tattoos where "good enough" just isn't good enough? I would add financial advice to the list. I know I'm biased, but some things simply demand a higher level of excellence.

In this chapter, I'm going to show you what "suitable" looks like in the financial services business and how this "suitability" allows conflicts of interest to exist. Like I said in the previous chapter, their satisfaction with what's "suitable" was exactly why I couldn't stand working for Wall Street mega-brokers.

THE RISE OF INVESTING AS WE KNOW IT

As I mentioned in Chapter 1, the 1970s saw much change in the investment business. Trading commissions were deregulated, giving rise to discount brokers such as Charles Schwab and TD Ameritrade. This cheaper access to financial markets was great for individual investors, but the brokerage business began to feel pressure as people were finding much less expensive ways to execute their self-directed transactions. As a result, brokerage firms like

EF Hutton started using a new, all-inclusive fee structure in what they called "managed accounts" or "wrap
accounts" whereby they leveraged the use of "exclusive"
investment managers whose percentage fee was simply a
portion of the overall fee (this is what large institutions
["smart money"] like CalPERS and the Teacher Retirement System of Texas [TRS] use to manage their billions
of dollars). Brokerage firms created a need for themselves
by offering this "institutional-style investing" to individual investors. The pitch was essentially that individual
investors should be managing their money like the smart
money does. Predictably, people bought in.

Institutional-style investing fixed several problems within
the brokerage firms. One was overactive broker trading
incentivized by commissions, also known as churning.
Recurring fee revenue from wrap accounts diminished
the brokerage firms' need for aggressive trading, and as
a by-product, the brokerage business seemingly became
more client-centric, boosting social rapport.

The transition brought in consistent and repeatable
revenue. This cash flow increased the share price of brokerage companies and reduced the pressure on brokers
who might have otherwise felt the need to supplement
their earnings by completing transactions at the end of
the month. Everyone felt they were winning, and so the
institutional style of money management began to per-

meate the individual investor marketplace in the early 1980s, where it remains prevalent today. Although this new management style was better than churning, it also had its own set of problems for clients.

In short, these managed accounts were still trading too much. Mom-and-pop investors generally don't know that extra activity generates extra taxes and erodes compounding of returns. When they execute more trades, they think they're getting what the big boys are getting, and they are excited to be "part of the game." However, large institutions such as state pensions, endowments, and foundations are tax-exempt (or at least tax-deferred) and the transactions created by managing the trades don't have any direct tax impact. This is not so for the typical mom-and-pop investor, who benefits from *less* activity, not more, occurring in their account. Not to mention, institutional money managers who call on those pensions and endowments do so for a discount that isn't offered to the typical mom-and-pop investor. And the difference can be staggering, often nearly 10 times the cost. These services are made very cheap for large investors and quite expensive for smaller ones. Smaller investors end up paying for services that have little mathematical probability of generating the returns necessary to cover the cost of the fees and taxes.

Further, decision makers at a large institution, such as

the board members of TRS, are responsible for hiring investment managers to manage the institution's retirement funds. They have a good reason for hiring out the management of those funds: reputation protection. They want the ability to blame somebody else if the stock market falls apart, and the members of the institution say, "How come you didn't protect my money by doing this or that?" The board members of TRS can always reply, "What did you want us to do? We hired Goldman Sachs!" The reputation insurance and insulation from criticism, along with a little liability relief, provides additional incentive to hand responsibility off to these professionals.

Brokers who hire a smart money manager on behalf of individual investors have the same goal in mind: to protect their reputations. In hiring a money manager, brokers are asking their clients to bear the burden of those additional fees (even as this arrangement greatly diminishes the brokers' workload). This allows the broker to carry the banner when performance is strong and burn the flag when performance is called into question, saying, "You're right, this manager is underperforming. Let's fire them and hire another." Individual investors are the ones who would directly benefit from less-expensive investment solutions. Yet, they are kept in this revolving-door system of hiring and firing investment managers, which ultimately obfuscates the fact that their performance will almost always trail the market because of the high costs. Membership in the exclusive smart money club may come with some bragging rights, but at what cost?

FOOL'S GOLD

The "smart money" club has several different iterations. When I worked at EF Hutton, the firm's top producers in the wrap business were treated like gods. The very top ones were even inducted into a club called the Alchemist Society, whose members were called Senior Alchemists.

Anne Marie Helmenstine, PhD, says this about alchemy: "Before chemistry was a science, there was alchemy. One of the supreme quests of alchemists was to transmute (transform) lead into gold. Lead (atomic number 82) and gold (atomic number 79) are defined as elements by the number of protons they possess. Changing the element requires changing the atomic (proton) number. The number of protons in an element cannot be altered by any chemical means. However, physics may be used to add or remove protons and thereby change one element into another. Because lead is stable, forcing it to release three protons requires a vast input of energy, so much so that the cost of transmuting it greatly surpasses the value of any resulting gold."

The alchemy that brokerage firms attempted was similarly futile. Brokers sold clients the idea of turning lead into gold, then charged them exorbitantly for the magical transformation, no matter that the client could have bought the gold (beta) themselves, for a much lower price.

So if individual investors excuse lagging performance, what do they actually value? It's not the fancy stock picking and the stimulation of playing the game; it's the handholding, problem-solving, strategy-developing, plan-implementing benefit of having a broker or financial advisor by their side. Investors want someone to tell them what they should do and someone to lean on when the stock market falls apart. If the services an investor truly desires are provided regardless of whether they are paying an outside manager, who is really reaping the benefit of paying extra for "smart money managers" and by how much?

CASH COWS

Let's dig into fees and client costs. The brokerage eco-system has fees, commissions, product costs, markups, spreads, and other structures to ensure that clients pay. These costs add up, but the client often doesn't know where their money goes or how their broker or advisor gets paid, nor how much goes to the firm.

We'll start by identifying the two main compensation structures you might have for each account in your household:[7] commissionable or fee-bearing. An account can have only one specific compensation structure. (I have seen clients in the past who had both structures repre-

---

7   Household as it is used here refers to the aggregation of all accounts owned by an investor or couple regardless of style or number of accounts, including IRAs, single, joint name, and so on.

sented in their household, just in different accounts, which proved to be a source of confusion.)

Commissions are a pretty straightforward compensation model. Your broker calls you up, recommends a trade, and tells you the cost. You either approve or don't. Hiring a broker who gets paid by commission seems like a fair deal. You think, *They get paid for the work they do. Sounds about right.* We've talked about how this has historically opened the floodgates for overtrading.

Fee-only accounts provide advice without the influence of product or per-trade commission. These fees can be flat or percentage based. What people often neglect to consider is that investment products themselves also have fees embedded. Mutual funds, ETFs, and other packaged products are not all the same, and the costs vary widely. Packaged products quote an expense ratio (the administrative costs of the fund) but may neglect to mention what that really means. Sometimes "administrative costs" go beyond actual management costs and include things such as the fund's advertising to other potential investors. You also need to know if there will be a transaction fee and whether you will pay a commission when you buy (front-end load[8]) or when you sell (back-end load[9]). Some of the costs are reasonable, but don't be afraid to ask for the full scoop. It all adds up.

Markups and spreads are another unforeseen cost. Let's say your broker is helping you buy IBM shares. He makes the purchase and gets a commission. It's a straightforward transaction. But what if you want to buy something unlisted, like a municipal bond? A brokerage firm might use their own money to buy the bonds for $290,000 and then turn around and sell them to clients for $300,000, profiting $10,000. The distinction is in the buy; they put their own money at risk and so own either the profit or the loss. It's not the typical broker position of matching the buyer and seller. Instead, they become a middleman who profits from the spread. It's also possible, though not common, to do this with listed securities, as long as the price is in range of the going rate. As you can see, it's complicated.

But what complicates things all the more and sheds light on the major possibility for conflicts of interest is that the broker is incentivized to use products that build fees and expenses into portfolios because the broker only gets paid

8   A front-end load is the mutual fund structure that pays commissions to brokers under FINRA regulations whereby principal is withdrawn up front from fund purchasers and returned to brokerage dealers as a sales commission.

9   A back-end load is a penalty levied against investors who liquidate before they reach a predefined holding period in order to recover commissions paid up front to a broker.

after her brokerage firm has taken a large piece of the pie. What if a broker wants to give a discount to a loyal client? Think again.

If the broker finds a way to reduce the fees for her client, her payout gets reduced first and disproportionately. If they give away too much to the client by reducing fees, the firm charges the broker for the loss in an effort to keep her in line as a valuable part of the profit-making machine. Truthfully, it is not the intent of every broker to overcharge their clients. The ecosystem is simply built on the idea of expanding the fee pool, and if the broker doesn't do that, she gets penalized.

To understand this, you have to think about the fact that tens of thousands of employees are monitoring the firm's business, looking to make the business more profitable, minding all of the compliance details, but never directly generating any revenue. The non-revenue-generating personnel wake up in the morning thinking about the revenue generators, the brokers. Why? Because their paycheck depends on it. Their value as an employee increases to the extent they contribute to the revenue-generating side of the business. The entire ecosystem, which the non-revenue generators designed, is set up to concoct ways to get brokers to do more business, more profitably. You end up with a giant ecosystem looking to do one thing: feed the beast. And if something doesn't feed the beast, they're not doing it.

When I worked for Paine Webber, they had frequent dog-and-pony shows during which upper-level managers shared how the firm was doing. They talked about how the competition (other large brokerage firms) was looking, how the independent advisor channel was growing (though they always diminished the value of this since it posed a threat), and which commissionable products brokers should be presenting to clients.

Each of these product presentations would contain three things:

1. A catalyst—every product needed something that inspired the client to act immediately. Clients who took time to "think about it" were a deadweight to your business. You wanted clients who were decision makers. You had to call the client and talk them into doing something, and so the key was to design products and services that had catalysts built into them. "It's only going to be available until next Thursday, Mr. Jones; you need to decide."
2. A promise of what's called alpha generation—every product proposed an "angle" to achieve either excess returns relative to the benchmark or reduced risk with a disproportionately high rate of possible return. We'll revisit this topic later in this chapter.
3. A glittery depiction of the math—every product would

derive a fee from the client, presented as "yield to broker" (commissions). Then the pitchman would flaunt how wonderful this would be without considering how a client would make money after their expenses were paid.

Some products had awful math, others not as bad, but all products would pay the broker to pitch them as long as the client said okay.

At one meeting, the troop of 300 brokers in Houston were summoned to hear my boss's boss speak. He went over various business metrics, inspired optimism in the troops, and reinforced what a great business this was and how lucky we were to work for such a fine firm. The boss man concluded his talk and introduced the room to a product guy who came on stage to tell us about his fancy new product that we fine men at this fine firm should pitch to our fine clients. His pitch went a little like this: "Listen, fellas, we've got this brilliant product to sell your clients. It's going to be fantastic!"

In short, this product was an index fund that mirrored the Standard & Poor's 500 stock index (S&P 500), minus the 50 names that the product designers thought were awful choices. They were going to derive their "alpha" from the 450 names that were better in their eyes. This could work occasionally, but the costs would have to be very low, as in under 0.5 percent, and the designers would have to be particularly lucky on some big negative events happening for only those 50 names. Frankly, there's no way these product guys were going to know which 50 of the 500 were going to be awful choices anyway, and surely some of the 50 that they chose to expunge were likely to end up being top performers. So this was clearly a commission-generating machine, not a performance machine.

Here's the takeaway: the odds of outperforming the market through products like these are near zero. Thanks to their structure, these products will simply garner a market return. And that's fine as long as the fees are low.

My jaw hit the floor when this lug nut told us the client fees were 4 percent. Remember that long-term returns from stocks are ~8 percent,[10] so half of the possible returns were going to fees in this case.

And on top of that, the product had a one-year life, after which the client had to liquidate. This meant gains were realized, and then taxes had to be paid. The client then would pay another fat fee when he got pitched on reinvesting the proceeds. "Mr. Jones, look at how well you did; let's buy the next one." Clearly, they built the product specifically to force it back to cash and to later force the client into another decision, which would include another theo-

---

10   Around 8 percent is based on the S&P 500 total return between the years 1960 and 2019.

retical catalyst, with lofty projections and underwhelming prospects.

Let's dig deeper into the math. The product creators would take nearly 40 percent of the revenue (1.5 percent of the 4 percent) for their bright idea and their department's work. The remaining 2.5 percent would go to the broker's pay grid.[11] The firm would then take 55 percent of the remaining 2.5 percent from the grid, leaving the broker with 1.125 percent, roughly one-fourth of the 4 percent fee. The firm then had the nerve to call that a 45 percent payout to the broker (1.125 ÷ 2.5 = 45 percent, but 1.125 ÷ 4 = 28 percent) because they like to overlook the fact that the broker gets skimmed twice. Calling it 45 percent acknowledges only one skim.

---

11 The pay grid is the spreadsheet that sorts out the broker's cut.

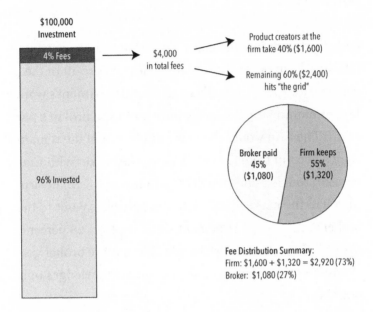

Fee Breakdown

$100,000 Investment

4% Fees

$4,000 in total fees

Product creators at the firm take 40% ($1,600)

Remaining 60% ($2,400) hits "the grid"

96% Invested

Broker paid 45% ($1,080)

Firm keeps 55% ($1,320)

Fee Distribution Summary:
Firm: $1,600 + $1,320 = $2,920 (73%)
Broker: $1,080 (27%)

I was offended by the pitch on multiple levels. I was offended for my own sake but *really* offended on behalf of the clients because there was just no way they could come out ahead.

Everyone else in the room was excited about it because the 4 percent fee looked juicy and they couldn't see how crazy this was. Then the product pitchman asked if there were any questions. Of course, being the muckraker I am, I raised my hand. I said, "Correct me if I'm wrong, but it looks to me like you've made an index fund that has the potential rate of return of, say 8 percent, over time, like all index funds.

You're taking 1.5 percent to give to the product designer who designed this piece of genius work. The remaining 2.5 percent is going to go to my grid where the firm will take another 55 percent of that, and I will get what's left. This means 75 percent of the revenue will stay at the firm, and the client is going to be robbed of any chance of making money because the fee is essentially consuming half of the potential returns. Mathematically, those 50 'stinker stocks' the product removed would have to be underperforming by at least 40 percent to justify the 4 percent fee the firm is charging in exchange for this new product. Is that correct?"

The product manager looked at me and said, "Um, well, I guess you could look at it that way."

As soon as I got to the office the next morning, my boss called me and asked me to meet him in his office. I walked down the hall and sat in the chair across from his desk. Immediately, he looked up and said, "So we'd really appreciate it if you didn't ask those types of tough questions in front of the group. It's like you created a big fart in the room and polluted the air for everyone else. Now nobody is going to sell that product to their clients."

I stood up, rested my knuckles on his desk as I leaned over, and said, "Well, tell those product designers to quit making such crappy funds and then I won't have to point it out in front of everybody."

He said, "Hey, look, if the firm makes money and you make money, two out of three ain't bad."

KEEPING THE POT STIRRED

While the math shakes out to be pretty bogus, there's a strong temptation to play dumb when you're in the broker's seat. The brokers all sit in a room and are pitched products that scratch itching ears. They are "advocates" for their clients to get what they want and "ambassadors" for brokerage firms to make deals. Clients want products "without stinkers." Firms want to sell products "without stinkers." When the products are "painted prettily" and fulfill what clients think they want, brokers don't look behind the curtain. It's more of a marketing game, not an investment game. They're just keeping the pot stirred.

It's like a buffet. The firm provides a plethora of options for the brokers to choose from. The broker takes his filled plate to offer the client a selection. If the client says, "Well, I like citrus fruit," the broker's going to put that on his plate. So the firm creates a smorgasbord for clients to choose from. Even though a plate of index funds would be far and away the best choice for the client, the firm doesn't offer that, only variations that have twists and big commissions. Why? A plate of index funds wouldn't generate much for the firm. That's why they put end dates on products and design products offering the chance at excess return. My boss would say, "The last thing you want in your clients' accounts are dormant assets." Brokerage firms produce internal reports on dormancy to identify "opportunities." They want to fertilize the turf so they can harvest more next year. They want the products to recycle themselves. That is the typical broker's job: nip gains while they're small to keep those dollars in play. Generate transactions so the firm can earn commission revenue. Ultimately, keep the pot stirred.

FUELING THE GREED

The thing is, clients like the action. When a broker pitches the advantage to be gained, showing clients the algorithms and the illusion of the upper hand, clients love the complexity. And clients super love believing they've found the guy smart enough to unlock it all. It's almost like a little magic black box. You put it all in, shake it all up, and bam! You got yourself a magic trick.

Let's go back to the casino analogy. People don't go to Vegas just to win. People go to Vegas to play the game. They hope to come out ahead but walk in knowing that if they lose money, at least they'll gain entertainment.

What investors don't realize is that Wall Street exploits the same human tendencies Vegas does. People get entertainment value from investing, but they also expect to win at it, at least occasionally. The problem with "entertaining" investors is that unlike a gambler in Vegas, an investor often has more than $1,000 on the line. They may even have their life savings up for ante.

Knowing this, Wall Street has its light show ready to mesmerize. Brokers say they can predict what tomorrow will look like. They carefully wordsmith the story to get you to sign on the dotted line. They know exactly how to play their cards to fuel the greed.

HOLD THE CHEESE

We don't have enough information to know what's going to happen tomorrow. Yes, people get lucky, but let's talk about overall portfolio performance.

At the core, the risk of participating in the market is simply called beta. If the market is up 1 percent, and 100 percent of your investable funds are in the market (a beta measure of 1.0), you should expect your account to be up 1 percent as well. If, instead, you have 50 percent of your investments in bonds, cash, or other non-market-correlating assets, then you're not taking market risk on that portion, and those allocations reduce your beta. If the market is up 1 percent, maybe your portfolio is up by 0.5 percent, and thus you've reduced your beta to 0.5.

You might hear a money manager say, "I can provide you something more than beta! If you put your money where I tell you to, I can provide you a higher return level." But they won't guarantee that, of course. It's all conceptual, back-tested, and hypothetical. Maybe it will materialize; maybe it won't. And I'll tell you in a minute why it's liable not to, but that "extra" is the concept of alpha.

Alpha can be experienced in a couple of different ways. One is by getting the same return as the market while taking on less risk. Another is by taking the same risk as the market and achieving a higher rate of return. But is alpha repeatable? Is it merely luck? Is it excessive risk taking that just hasn't gone bad *yet*?

Every money manager adheres to a methodology. For example, one manager might say, "We buy small companies, and they have to show a certain growth rate over time." Another might say, "We buy only big companies, but they have to pay a dividend and have low debt-to-equity." That's really only a filter, not a decision-making process. All they're doing is narrowing down the universe from which they select securities for their strategy. However, most portfolio decision making does not lead to alpha generation. Brokers merely use the idea of alpha to get people to pay for extra services. The concept of alpha is what most people selling investment management services focus on: delivering excess returns.

CAN ANYONE GAIN ALPHA?

Although it's generally difficult to gain an advantage, there are always exceptions. It's just that not everybody is entitled to one. If you build a portfolio full of the exceptions you think you deserve, you will often be sorely disappointed. You should build a buffer into your portfolio so that you can isolate your attempts at alpha.

One way to gain alpha is in private equity. You obtain something different in private equity that you cannot get in the public securities marketplace: the inherent discount for the illiquidity of a non-publicly traded company.

I think any money manager who rides on his ability to generate alpha should be willing to get paid only for the alpha he generates. Advisors, including those at my current firm, don't get paid based on whether they can generate alpha both because they don't have confidence that they'll be able to generate it, and because they are delivering other value-added services separate from alpha. If they're not confident in their ability it's because excess return often depends on factors outside of the advisors' control, and the entire community loathes admitting that. They want to convince you of how smart they are so they can tack on commissions and fees, which make excess returns even more elusive. Just to be clear, I'm not talking out of both sides of my mouth here; my firm does not pitch our ability to generate market-beating returns on a client's investments, but we *do* thrive by generating returns in excess of those advisors who say they can beat the market. How? Because we don't earn commissions or charge insane fees. We know we can rise to the top of the heap simply because methodologies that attempt alpha generation have such high costs and our costs are so low.

Every year, S&P publishes a scorecard called the *SPIVA Report*, which reviews money managers, categorized by methodology, and compares them to each other and the benchmark (100 percent beta) for that same grouping. The vast majority of managers consistently underperform. There is routinely a narrow subset that outperforms, but research shows that few are able to repeat that outperformance in the subsequent year. S&P also produces a report called the *Persistence Scorecard*, and in 2019, the report concluded that "less than 3% of equity funds in all categories maintained their top-quartile status at the end of the five-year measurement period. In fact, no large-cap fund was able to consistently deliver top-quartile performance by the end of the fifth year."[12] As the saying goes, "Even a broken clock is right twice a day." Any money manager who sticks to his knitting is going to have the stars align at some point. Lo and behold, the year he's able to do that will be shown on the marketing materials he presents to you just to show how smart he is.

---

12 "Does Past Performance Matter? The Persistence Scorecard," S&P Dow Jones Indices, December 2019.

In 2018, stocks that paid high dividends were shunned because interest rates were rising, and those stocks had a relative disadvantage. But what happened in 2019 when interest rates were falling? The value of that cash flow was suddenly greater, and those stocks outperformed. Any manager with a dividend-focused methodology in 2018 had a natural disadvantage; holding the exact same securities in 2019 suddenly provided an advantage. That's the alignment of the stars I'm talking about. From one year to the next, the same strategy yielded much different results, mostly thanks to external factors.

Bill Miller is the Legg Mason Value Trust Fund manager who gained notoriety for beating the market for 15 straight years. Afterward, he said this: "As for the so-called streak, that's an accident of the calendar. If the year ended on different months, it wouldn't be there, and at some point, the mathematics will hit us. We've been lucky. Well, maybe it's not 100% luck—maybe 95% luck." Michael Mauboussin, the former chief investment strategist at Legg Mason Capital Management, studied the historical data of that same time period and confirmed Miller's assessment. Mauboussin discovered that the percentage of equity mutual funds that beat the market during Value Trust's 15-year streak was as low as 8 percent in one year and 13 percent in another. He estimated the probability of beating the market in the 15 years ending 2005 was 1 in 2.3 million.

The fact of the matter is, this alpha concept eludes actual investor results more than 90 percent of the time.[13]

It's like walking into a restaurant known for its cheeseburger and taking a seat at your table all excited for the experience. The waitress walks up and says, "All righty, folks! We have two things on the menu today: a hamburger and a cheeseburger!" To which you ask, "What's the price difference?"

"Well, honey, the hamburger is $1.50, and the cheeseburger is $9.20."

"But the hamburger has the same bun? All the same lettuce and tomato minus the cheese?"

"Yup, but there's one more thing you need to know if you order the cheeseburger. You're paying the upcharge for cheese, but there's also a 90 percent chance your burger won't come out with cheese on it."

"So let me get this straight. You're saying there's a 90 percent chance my $9.20 cheeseburger won't show up with cheese on it?"

"Yes, but, honey, it's the best cheese!"

---

13   S&P Global and Berlinda Liu, *SPIVA® U.S. Year-End 2019* (n.p.: S&P Dow Jones Indices, 2020), https://www.spglobal.com/spdji/en/spiva/article/spiva-us-year-end-2019.

If I were at this restaurant, I'd say, give me a hamburger and please hold the cheese. Likewise, when 90 percent of investors never see alpha and when the cost of alpha is greater than the benefit you can derive from it, you're better off going for beta. The fees to simply participate in beta are roughly 0.15 percent, or $1.50 in cheeseburger vernacular. The typical cost of the average active stock mutual fund is about six times that, or 0.92 percent[14] according to Morningstar,[15] or roughly $9.20 in the cheeseburger example. Who would ever order the cheeseburger?

Although brokers present themselves as the key to unlocking complexity, investors can buy these kinds of filters at a much lower cost in more ways than one. It may give people comfort to know that someone else made the selection for them, but if you're able to cut the fluff, you're more likely to generate alpha investing on your own simply because you won't pay a fee. If you want an advisor to be responsible for it all, both of you would be better off on an independent platform that doesn't carry the cost baggage and crossed-up allegiances of any major brokerage firm.

---

14 This number accounts for the fact that many mutual funds include a 12b-1 fee (whereas ETFs do not). Once you take the 0.670 percent and add in the kickback, 0.95 percent is about right. These costs have made strides. I remember when the number was more like 1.25 percent.

15 Morningstar, Inc., Ben Johnson, and Adam McCullough, "U.S. Fund Fee Study: Investors Saved an Estimated $5.5 Billion in Fund Fees in 2018," Morningstar.com, 2019, https://www. morningstar.com/.

2020: NEW SEC REGULATIONS

On June 30, 2020, the Securities and Exchange Commission (SEC) began enforcing what is known as Regulation Best Interest,[16] or in the brokerage industry, Reg BI. Legislators who had endured much finger-pointing and blaming in the aftermath of the 2008 downdraft were motivated to further tighten the framework of broker-client interaction to ensure the clients' "best interest." The brokerage community–and the lobbyists they paid–fought the passage of Reg BI tooth and nail. A dictum forcing the fiduciary standard across the board would have wide-reaching implications, most often harming smaller individual investors. That's because you won't find an advisor who is willing to accept fiduciary responsibility for small accounts. There's just not enough financial reward. The SEC knew this, and that's why they wrangled with it for nearly a decade. The result? A requirement that advisors *attempt* to reduce conflicts, unless, of course, they can't. We can now expect brokerage firms to play this up to their favor presenting themselves as "essentially fiduciary."

This rule amounts to "fiduciary lite" because brokerage firms are still allowed to operate on commissions and keep kickbacks from mutual fund companies, and they can still keep backroom side deals with other providers as long as they disclose these actions in a client distributed form called Form Client Relationship Summary (Form CRS). This form must be distributed to clients at the inception of any new account, and annually thereafter, and cannot exceed two pages in length, ostensibly to increase the odds that it's actually read.

---

16 Securities and Exchange Commission, *Regulation Best Interest: The Broker-Dealer Standard of Conduct*, 2019, https://www.govinfo.gov/content/pkg/FR-2019-07-12/pdf/2019-12164.pdf.

Reg BI has four primary obligations that brokerage firms must satisfy:

1. **Disclosure Obligation**—providing investors with all facts relating to the scope and terms of their relationship with a broker/advisor, including conflicts of interest that may arise with recommendations. Presenting Form CRS to clients satisfies most of this obligation.

2. **Care Obligation**—requiring brokers/advisors to at least understand the risks and costs of investments presented to clients, among those offered by the brokerage firm. It does not, however, require the brokerage firm to offer the cheapest alternatives.

3. **Conflict-of-Interest Obligation**—requiring that conflicts of interest be mitigated when possible; when this is not possible, a disclosure must suffice.

4. **Compliance Obligation**—requiring the brokerage firm to establish internal policies and procedures to ensure that brokers/advisors are complying with items 1-3 above.

While the SEC's adoption document[17] is 184 pages long, the first six pages tell you everything you need to know about it. I found this language on page 5 particularly insightful: "We [SEC] have declined to subject broker-dealers to a wholesale and complete application of the existing fiduciary standard under the Advisers Act because it is not appropriately tailored to the structure and characteristics of the broker-dealer business model." No kidding. I would also

---

17   Securities and Exchange Commission, *Regulation Best Interest: The Broker-Dealer Standard of Conduct*, 2019, https://www.govinfo.gov/content/pkg/FR-2019-07-12/pdf/2019-12164.pdf.

recommend you read the Form CRS of your brokerage firm and see for yourself if it sounds like it's designed as a client-first document or as a shield/CYA.

Anyhow, this new standard of conduct was designed to change some of the ways things work. Yet, as you can see from the Reg BI rule book quoted above, most conflicts can still be simply disclosed and not resolved. Many of the new rules will allow the suitability standard to survive and may only generate additional confusion as to how "fiduciary lite" makes any sense. We will see if this causes brokerages to pivot, or if it inspires no change at all.

CHAPTER FOUR

———

CHECK YOURSELF

"Truth—more precisely, an accurate understanding of reality—is the essential foundation for producing good outcomes."

—RAY DALIO, BUSINESSMAN, AUTHOR, BILLIONAIRE

I hate to break it to you, but you aren't off the hook. Considering what we talked about in the first part of this book, there is absolutely no doubt Wall Street's operations lead to an inordinate amount of pain and frustration for their clients, including you. But a certain amount of honest introspection here will be very valuable. So how about a little heart to heart? Not between the two of us but between you and yourself. If you can honestly and accurately assess who you are and what you want, you will save yourself from a world of trouble. And the cherry on top is that those who are willing to take this honest look at themselves typically end up with money that formerly belonged to those who refuse to do so. That's because the stock market is a somewhat closed ecosystem, wherein one group stands to benefit from the mistakes of another. In this chapter, we are going to unpack a bit of behavioral science that will help us keep our self-harm tendencies in check.

Looking back at your financial road, many decisions have led to where you stand at this moment. If you're like most investors, a number of years ago, you stumbled across someone on the golf course who happened to be a broker at one of the big brokerage firms. Turns out, he's your cousin's best friend's husband. And the story he told you tickled your ears. His strategies sounded like they would bring in a pretty penny and resolve your financial problems and anxieties. So you opened an account with him. After months or years working with this guy, you realized your returns were subpar, given the risk you were taking. He always seemed to be explaining why each rise in value was due to his remarkable intelligence while each fall was market-related and out of his control. The guy is likely just as good at perception management as he is at money management. And you got left hangin'. You might have tried again with another buddy's buddy and had a similar experience. Perhaps you spent some time mulling over the details of what happened and resolved to "never let that happen again."

But as I see it, the disappointment you felt both times might have as much (or more) to do with your own tendencies and expectations as with your broker's/advisor's shortfalls. Further, most of the problems investors encounter are rooted in an inaccurate assessment of their own relationship with money. In order to take a look under the hood, we have to consult some basics of the psychology behind investing.

WE ARE BIASED

Investor psychology is a life's work, worthy of its own PhD program. Although I have decades of experience interacting with investors making decisions, I by no means claim to be an expert in investing psychology or behavioral economics. But I'll bring in a few guys who are. My personal favorite is Daniel Kahneman. If you want to dive into his work, be prepared to be amazed by the theories he dedicated his life to studying and proposing to the world. His work with Amos Tversky guided most of the current ways we understand decision making. It's no surprise he received the Nobel Prize in 2002 (Tversky passed in 1996) for "their integrated insights from psychological research into economics, especially concerning human judgment and decision-making under uncertainty." And since uncertainty (unknown unknowns) and risk (known unknowns) are what we are up against with investing, we'd be wise to listen to what he and Tversky had to say.

When Kahneman and Tversky published their theory "Judgement under Uncertainty: Heuristics and Biases,"[18] they gained attention around the world. Rightly so. Uncertainty is a universal foe. Myriad unknowns cause fear-based thoughts, which cause countless sleepless nights and self-damaging responses.

Prior to Kahneman and Tversky's work, economists assumed investors were able to correctly estimate probabilities, putting their human biases aside to make fully rational decisions. It was assumed that any errors in estimation were surely outliers. Those earlier economic models of decision making assumed decision makers to be patient, enduring, rational, and even-keeled. They assumed people could assess the desirability and likelihood of potential outcomes and funnel their information through a calculated filter that would then lead to the optimal decision. But who are we kidding? Investors are human and are certainly not immune to biases.

Consider confirmation bias and the power it gives people to selectively interpret information in favor of their preexisting beliefs. How about cognitive ease? This bias dictates how willing we are to spend time on a topic or activity based solely on how easily we understand it. If a question is too complicated, our substitution bias would have

---

18   Amos Tversky and Daniel Kahneman, "Judgement under Uncertainty: Heuristics and Biases," *Science*, n.s., 185, no. 4157 (1974): 1124–1131, https://www.jstor.org/stable/1738360.

us substitute the question altogether for a simpler one. There's also the narrative bias where we see the world as a coherent story. If a new fact doesn't fit our narrative, it can't be true. All of these biases and the continually evolving list of them hold undeniable sway in our lives.

Remember what a disaster 2008 was? A few weeks into that mess, a friend and client of mine called me at five o'clock in the morning. He had been up since two, pacing, trying to stomach the possibility of "the market never recovering" because the majority of his nest egg was tied up in it. He had already consulted his biases and jumped to the end of the story in his mind; he wanted to fix it, to make moves. He wanted to do something to get rid of the racing thoughts, the heart palpitations, and the pit in his stomach. But there was no move to be made at the time. He didn't have any insights, only angst caused by information overload and a racing mind thinking about how much worse it could get. I told him to sit still.

Kahneman and Tversky's findings show that "people rely on a limited number of heuristic principles which reduce the complex tasks of assessing probabilities and predicting values to simplify judgmental operations." Heuristics are shortcuts stemming from a system of thinking by reference. They're most often associated with a successive system, such as "If A, then B, so C must be next." Consequently, under uncertainty, humans quickly jump to conclusions often associated with worst-case scenarios. Often, the more dire the perceived circumstance, the further down the line we end up when we jump to conclusions. We do this to truncate the time it takes to decide what to do, but it can lead to exponential miscalculations. We inaccurately measure and estimate all kinds of things, and it turns out, we do so rather predictably. In many ways, both experience and research show we are our own worst enemies.

Many people called it quits in '08. They were impatient and irrational. Why? In the face of uncertainty, they subconsciously fell into the three heuristics that Kahneman and Tversky pointed out: representativeness, availability, and adjustment from an anchor. Let's go one by one.

Representativeness: In short, this means people assume what "looks like ___" will also end up "looking like ___." It's like the phrase that physicians are taught in their diagnostic training: "When you hear hooves, think horse, not zebra." They're told this because it's most likely that a patient has the most common problem. Yet, with investing, this assumption can lead to a lot of big mistakes. For example, a market high *can* happen right before a recession. But a market high can also continue to go up and stay up. You might be tempted to anticipate the former, believing what goes up must come down. And you could be totally wrong.

Availability: This refers to the ease with which an example comes to mind. This can help us make fast assessments, yet just because we can quickly think of a handful of examples of our biggest fears, doesn't mean the worst is about to happen.

Adjustment from an anchor: In short, this means people get stuck on their initial starting point when moving into making their decisions. An anchor, used properly, can help people process their situation based on a familiar point. However, an anchor can do to you exactly what it does to a boat: hold you down.

WE ARE IRRATIONAL

Another of my favorite behavioral scientists, Richard Thaler, won the 2017 Nobel Memorial Prize in Economic Sciences for his work in identifying humans as "predictably irrational" when making economic decisions.

Any economist would agree that humans can be irrational, but as I mentioned above, the standard school of thought would claim humans to be rational overall, with any irrationality being the exception and not the rule. Like Kahneman, Thaler took things a step further to give us principles and predictive models that have very relevant implications to what we are discussing here.

If humans were rational with their money, they would

always act in their best interest. But Thaler's studies[19] confirmed that we really don't do that. The way he explains our "predictable irrationality" is quite simple. He points out that we are "mental accounters," which means we like to simplify our decision making by categorizing, sometimes leading ourselves to irrational conclusions. With our money, we categorize or classify and thus open ourselves up to counterproductive investment ideas. This is how people end up paying 18 percent on their credit card debt while managing "investments" that should instead be liquidated to pay off the debt, or how people view a $100 birthday check from grandma as spendable money rather than fungible income. It "feels better" to have money sectioned off where we can enjoy our credits and ignore our debits. We often promote this thinking even when we don't believe our own spiel, comforting ourselves by repeating ideas that couldn't stand up to scrutiny.

Thaler also found that we suffer from the "endowment effect," meaning that once we own something (or feel that we do), we irrationally overvalue it.[20] Kahneman also studied the endowment effect by conducting a simple coffee mug experiment. To the control group, he gave two one-dollar bills. To the other group, he gave a coffee

---

19 Richard Thaler, "Behavioral Economics: Past, Present, and Future," *The 2018 Ryerson Lecture*, May 14, 2018, https://www.youtube.com/watch?v=A1M9VSgsSW4.

20 Daniel Kahneman, Jack L. Knetsch, and Richard H. Thaler, "Anomalies: The Endowment Effect, Loss Aversion, and Status Quo Bias," *Journal of Economic Perspectives* 5, no. 1 (Winter 1991): 193–206.

mug, which had a retail value of two dollars. He asked the groups to interact and make an exchange transaction at some price. No exchanges took place because the mug owners overvalued the mugs so greatly that they would not accept the two-dollar retail price, which already contained a profit margin over the cost to manufacture. I have seen this effect play out personally in selling real estate. In many cases, we see our own property as sharing similarities with the best properties in our neighborhood. In my case, it was rational that the price of my property, the home we raised our kids in for 20 years, should have some deductions for its quirks. But I was reluctant to reckon with the fact that I valued the ownership of my property more than a potential new owner would.

This irrational attachment to what we already own can infect our thinking when it comes to investing, too. It takes keen peripheral vision to be aware that every position we own is at the exclusion of something else. We must remove the rose-colored glasses, get outside of our valuation of the things we own, and fairly review the purchases we've made in the past.

WE ARE EMOTIONAL

One last thing we can be sure of, and really must consider seriously, is the role our emotions play in decision making, especially risky decision making. Stanford professor Baba

Shiv, along with George Loewenstein and Antoine Bechara, published a study on the topic back in 2005.[21]

The study was called "The Dark Side of Emotion in Decision-Making: When Individuals with Decreased Emotional Reactions Make More Advantageous Decisions." The title itself intrigued me. In this study, the researchers tested the hypothesis from Shiv's previous research, where he used an "investment task" to simulate real-life investment decisions in terms of uncertainties, rewards, and punishments. The interesting twist in the study was that the participants were from two separate groups. One consisted of average Joes, and the other group was made up of patients with impaired but stable focal lesions in brain regions related to emotion. The lesion patients with abnormal emotional circuitry experienced less "myopic loss aversion"[22] and therefore made more advantageous decisions. These results suggest that "dysfunction in neural systems subserving emotion leads to reduced levels of risk aversion, and thus, leads to more advantageous decisions in cases where risk-taking is rewarded."[23]

---

21 Baba Shiv, George Loewenstein, and Antoine Bechara, "The Dark Side of Emotion in Decision-Making: When Individuals Make More Advantageous Decisions," *Cognitive Brain Research* 23 (2005): 85–92, https://www.cmu.edu/dietrich/sds/docs/loewenstein/DarkSideEmotionDM.pdf.

22 U. Gneezy and J. Potters, "An Experiment on Risk Taking and Evaluation Periods," *The Quarterly Journal of Economics* 112, no. 2 (May 1997): 631–645.

23 B. Shiv, G. Loewenstein, A. Bechara, H. Damasio, and A. R. Damasio, "Investment Behavior and the Negative Side of Emotion," *Psychological Science* 16, no. 6 (2004): 435–439.

We intuitively understand this natural risk aversion about ourselves. This is the primary reason even the best individual investors hire professional advisors. Some advisors even hire advisors for themselves. Skilled advisors are often very good at telling others what to do with their money because they care less about the outcome. I often envision this dynamic as a duel in an old western movie. The one who snatches his gun and fires first without thinking is usually the victor. Aiming would not only give a time disadvantage, but it would also allow him some time to think of the enormity of his situation and start shaking. A shaky cowboy can't hit the broadside of a barn. Nerves of steel? Cool as a cucumber? Call it what you will, emotional detachment is advantageous under stress.

What does all of this mean? Our biases interfere with our decision making. Our irrational tendencies cause grave errors in judgment. Fear and greed influence our perceptions. When I think about these three realities, my own observations become strikingly clear. Leaning on our tendencies and preferences to aid us in decision making takes us away from facts, logic, and reason. After 35 years of counseling investors in tens of thousands of situations, I can say that my experience confirms the studies, and the studies confirm my experience.

Here are my top-10 observations:

1. WE THINK TOO HIGHLY OF OURSELVES.

Various studies report this statistic: two-thirds of investors consider themselves above average.[24] At the same time, their performance lags, and they inaccurately diminish the intelligence of those who are "surely doing worse." The truth is, you don't know what tomorrow will hold, you will not always be right, and you cannot have all of the best information all of the time nor act on it at just the right time and in just the right way. Your overconfidence will only lead to excessive trading, most often leading you to take the wrong action at the wrong time. The first behavioral economist, Adam Smith, said this overconfidence could be defined as "the overweening conceit which the greater part of men have of their own abilities."

2. WE HATE LOSSES MORE THAN WE LOVE WINS.

How sweet the smell of victory. We've all experienced it. We all talk about it. But what about losing? We talk about that far less even though it provokes a much stronger emotion. Kahneman's studies found that we hate losing three times more than we love winning. Adam Smith said, "Pain...is, in almost all cases, a more pungent sensation than the opposite and correspondent pleasure." Sure, we can get away with this loss aversion in surface-level con-

---

24 Gary Belsky, "Why We Think We Are Better Investors than We Think We Are," *The New York Times*, March 25, 2016, https://www.nytimes.com/2016/03/27/your-money/why-we-think-were-better-investors-than-we-are.html.

versations with our peers, but the reality ends up biting us when we refuse to make moves because we just might lose. This also explains why investors sell their winners and keep their losers despite the horrific math. They do this to get the self-gratification of a win while deferring the reality of a loss, which could always recover and confirm their stellar abilities.

3. WE ARE SKITTISH.

If you've ever been to a parade, you might have seen how skittish horses can be. With all of the people crowded on the sidelines, all of the eyes on them, all of the noises escalating, it makes them unpredictable. So it is with investors in the stock market. It creates an inordinate amount of noise when an investor watches a volatile line dictate the numbers in their account. They feel the weight of the eyes that could be on them, the crowd that could blame them for a bad decision. This weighs even heavier the more we have touted our abilities to our friends. We could lose face. Suddenly, investors are jumpy and unpredictable, and there's a high chance of bucking where someone is going to get hurt. British economist John Maynard Keynes said, "Day-to-day fluctuations in the profits of existing investments, which are obviously of an ephemeral and non-significant character, tend to have an altogether excessive, and even absurd, influence on the market."

4. WE GET WRAPPED UP IN THE WHAT-IF.

Let's take the lottery, for example. The odds of winning Powerball, the most popular interstate lottery, are the same as getting struck by lightning on your birthday. Many people are aware of how low the odds of winning are, yet they still go to check out at the gas station and see the lotto tickets as the key to fulfilling their dream of owning that Porsche 911 they've always wanted and becoming the envy of all their friends. So they go for it. If we were rational about odds, we would never buy a ticket because 99.999999 percent of people who buy lottery tickets lose 100 percent of their money.

In the same way, people repeatedly hear about a hot new stock pick that promises to fulfill their wildest dreams. Yet with picking stocks, there's more perceived control, skill, and smarts to claim, making our friends' envy all the more valuable. Although the likelihood of success might be a little higher than in the lottery, the odds are still no deterrent. People are impulsive. They want that Porsche 911. The what-if wins the day.

5. WE'RE PLAGUED BY FEAR AND GREED.

When the market goes down—fear. When the market is soaring—greed (we could call this one fear, too, but the fear of missing out). Over time, every investor will brush up against these two emotions, both of which are extremely powerful motivators.

If we take a look at any major downturn in the market, it won't take long to notice the fear that cripples investors. The dot-com bubble bursting back in the late 1990s is a great example. There was a mass abandonment of entire financial plans because people were scared, thinking their losses were only going to get more and more intolerable. Regardless of any previously established "long-term" plans to stick it out, millions of investors turned into turtles, pulling in their necks and flipping up their shell flap.

Greed, on the other hand, quickens investors to bite off more than they can chew. The tulip mania in the Netherlands back in the 1600s is one of the most well-known market crashes in history. The tulip was one of the most unique flowers people had ever seen. It was a luxury item, reserved for those at the top of the top. But, of course, the middle class wanted in on the action! Why should this status item be scarcely available to the common folk? Well, it was super difficult to keep alive. So people started cultivating tulips to sell, and a full-on market was developed around these unique flowers. Bulb prices skyrocketed. People were greedy for the action. They didn't want to miss out. But eventually, the price of the bulbs declined, and holders had to liquidate at the bottom when the market fell apart. Within three years or so, the bubble burst.

A similar frenzy happened in Texas in the late 1980s with ostriches and emus. Breeding pairs of emus were listed in the *Houston Chronicle* classifieds (pre-eBay!) for $25,000! Three years later, the ad read, "Come shoot an emu on my property: Only $50!"

I have seen this so many times. The market gyrates and shakes out those who are either spending too much time on the sidelines or those so eager to win they end up making rookie mistakes.

6. WE HAVE A SCARCITY MENTALITY.

For the most part, it is possible to view our financial situation through a lens of abundance, no matter how little money we have. Yet, so many of us fail to do so. We may say we are "blessed beyond measure," but in reality, so many people struggle to shake the fear of never having enough. This worldview of fear is referred to as the scarcity mentality, which cripples us and causes us to make decisions that are self-protective and premature. This can totally undermine our futures, and not just when it comes to finances but also in many other overindulgent practices that the American dream shamelessly generates: obesity, infidelity, you name it.

7. WE INVEST TO MAKE OURSELVES FEEL GOOD.

The great Wall Street fantasy purports that hard work, smarts, and a little luck are all you need to pick the right stocks at just the right time to beat the system. Unfortunately (for most), it doesn't quite work that way.

I once had a prospective client come to my office to show me his accounts, hoping I could help make sense of the mess he had made for himself. He had several million dollars at a discount brokerage and was actively managing it himself, although he innately knew he was just spinning his wheels. He subscribed to expensive newsletters and traveled the nation attending conferences, always looking for the next big thing. He had some wins, some losses, one big win, and one colossal loss. He repeated a common phrase that I often hear in reviews like this: "I've made money!" And he had, but all of his picks, losses and wins combined, had left him with a fourth of the return he could have had with broader market exposure and fewer trades.

The bigger problem for him was the emotional toll of not knowing what to do next. We walked through what it would look like for our team to manage his money, relieving him of the burden. He was ready to transfer his assets by the end of our meeting, but at the last minute, he tried to carve off a piece to keep the game going. I told him he sounded like a gambler in distress. He totally accepted the admonition and appreciated the candor. He transferred all of his assets and has never looked back.

Sometimes people have a small addiction to the adrenaline of the game. All they want is to feel good, to get up to that tee box, swing their 2 iron and say to their 3-man audience, "Yep, I got myself some Bitcoin." Trading hot ideas might sound fun and exciting, but it can be consuming, and in 35 years, I have never, ever seen any individual investor do it well.

8. WE ARE SHORTSIGHTED.

Adam Smith said, "The pleasure which we are to enjoy ten years hence interests us so little in comparison with that which we may enjoy today." Easier said than done. It takes a good bit of self-control to make choices that reveal the later pleasure as the greater one.

I had a client who bought $5,500 worth of Union Pacific stock back in 1974. He held it through thick and thin, watching the sleepy railroad drop in value by 50 percent and recover time and again. Many people would have been spooked, but not this guy. He believed in the value of what he was holding on to; he believed that rail had a low-cost monopoly on interstate cargo travel. And you know what? He was right. His $5,500 grew by 15,000 percent.

Fifteen-thousand percent!

He never reinvested dividends but took them as a bonus cash flow and let the value of his stock rise and fall as it may. When he died, we tallied his forty-two years of dividend income at slightly over $190,000—on a $5,500 investment! That did not include the market value of his many stock splits and 8,000 share balance, worth over $625,000 at his death. Every bit of the $619,500 profit ended up being tax-free, which I'll tell you more about in a bit. All the cagey stock trades in the world could not have kept up with forty-two years of his doing nothing.

This kind of long-term perspective is rare yet absolutely necessary. More often than not, it pays off.

9. WE ARE SELF-PROTECTIVE.

Fear of the unknown tends to paralyze its victims, sending us into survival mode, which can strip us of our objectivity and cause us to self-protect. This manifests in many ways when it comes to investing: be it the familiarity bias, where we forgo the benefits of diversification in order to "stick to what we know," or the reference point bias where we value ourselves or our choices in comparison to another person instead of independently, or the attachment bias when our judgment gets blurred by our own self-interest in an investment, or the confirmation bias where we ignore information that would make us feel bad about ourselves. There are more, but it's clear that we set up mental patterns, even mental blocks, in order to self-protect, and we become completely unobjective and consequently unsuccessful.

10. HINDSIGHT IS 20/20.

People are actually quite gracious with themselves, especially when it comes to a financial decision they made in the past. They look back and purport, with great clarity, their own genius, even if they were wrong. Famed investor Gary Brinson said, "Everything is murky out of the windshield but crystal clear in the rearview mirror." That's because our decision-making processes are fraught with emotional pitfalls. We are wired to see patterns that don't exist. We conduct research to confirm our own opinions, ensuring everything fits our own hero narrative. Some people spend a lifetime repeating the process only to claim ownership of the good and disown the bad, believing the whole system must be rigged against them.

IT'S OKAY TO BE EMOTIONAL

You might be overwhelmed right now if you identified with any number of the observations listed above. I get it; it's tough to swallow. But here's where people really go wrong.

They think, "Got it. Don't be emotional. I can do that." But that never works because being emotional is part of being human. Emotions are just instinctive states of mind that we conjure up subconsciously, drawing from our circumstances and experiences. It's what we do with those emotions that really matters.

For each of us, our relationship with money is unique and complex. We each come from different backgrounds, cultures, and families that inform how we perceive and interact with money. We equate money with power, love, control, and self-worth. And because money promises to meet all of our innate needs and desires and often fails to do so, it brings with it a load of emotion that is difficult to bear. Nevertheless, we choose to carry the heavy load and use different tactics as we keep running the race, trying to escape the fear of not having enough. The emotions your money evokes cannot be packaged neatly and tidily. But you can get past them. And you must.

Taming the beast of emotion is impossible, but taming our response to the beast is surely a worthy cause.

When I was 17, I worked at a hospital and put ten dollars a week into a savings account. Back then, the goal was to have enough money to buy parts for the 1972 Camaro I was fixing up. As I got older, my goals shifted, but I consistently forged strategies and disciplines to meet my financial needs. Thinking back on it, no matter what I was saving for, I was meticulous with the math because at my core, I could not shake the fear of not having enough. It makes sense because growing up with very little meant running out was a very real possibility. Yet, instead of letting the fear of running out lead me to a place of scarcity forever, I had to contextualize my trauma and use my experience as fuel to make better decisions. That meant that my thinking had to be clear.

Humans make all kinds of errors, many of which we could avoid if only we thought correctly.

CHAPTER FIVE

CHANGE YOUR MIND

"Knowledge comes from experience, but wisdom, that's the good stuff. And wisdom comes from bad experience."

—ROSS KYGER III, MD

The good news is, you can prepare your mindset to be successful. The first step is to understand what you're up against because there's no point in trying to hide from the boogeymen who haunt you. The question then becomes, what does a mindset change look like? The aim here is to develop the ability to digest trauma and not allow it to affect your next decision. As we learned in the last chapter about emotion and its vexing effects in accomplishing our goals, getting past how you feel about something often leads to better decision making. This is what puts superior investors in a category by themselves.

One of these superior investors was an old client and great friend of mine, the late Ross Kyger III (quoted above). Ross had tons of great qualities about him, the most endearing being how inherently reasonable he was. He claimed that came by way of a "lifetime of evaluating disappointment," which is exactly what made him such a great individual investor. He learned from the emotional frailties of other investors and saw that their generally unreasonable expectations would allow him great opportunities.

Even if you aren't as "inherently reasonable" as Ross, you too can develop this counterintuitive mentality, though the process is not easy. It involves serious introspection and adaptation. But the end result is invaluable: it keeps you from misery, the investing reality for so many people. They feel their situation is tenuous, they take on more risk than they should, they lose a large sum of money, their hopes and aspirations go up in flames.

Ask Theranos shareholders what they think about the blood-testing company that used fraudulent data to build a multibillion-dollar business. Their deceptive practices were found out and the entire company basically blew up. The shareholders walked away duped, damaged, and depleted.

Ask any Enron shareholders from 2001 what they thought about their $90 share price plummeting to less than $1 over a matter of months. Same deal.

These types of war stories get grouped together and lead us to believe that anything good will go bad and give credence to the stories about how dangerous stocks are to our net worth. All of which contribute to self-destructive tendencies, emotional distress, anxiety, and a host of potential problems investors find themselves dealing with—unless they learn a better way.

One of my company's most important practices is to coach people through the erasure of prior habits based on erroneous thinking and the desire to "beat the market." I've seen it all. Rather than diversifying, aiming to match the market with the fewest disadvantages, people swing for the fences over and over. Every time one of them gets up to the plate, they point their bat to the outfield and say, "This will make up for that Theranos deal," or deeper, "This one's for you, Dad!" (even long after Dad has passed), or broader, "This one's for all the times people thought I wasn't smart." The desire to make up for insecurities, wounds, and fears gets people wound up tightly as they make their way to bat. Here comes the pitch! Curveball. Swing and a miss.

Investors should prepare for curveballs before they even get up to the plate. They have to understand that the real game is played by bunting and hitting singles and even being willing to get hit by the ball once or twice. If you want to score runs, do it base by base. Unfortunately, most people want to stand up and swing hard at every pitch so they can be the next Babe Ruth and break all the home run records. But that isn't the way to win ball games. In the end, portfolios will stand the test of time by how many runs we score, not by how many home runs we hit.

So, there is hope. You can hold a philosophy and perspective that will give you the confidence to get out of the dugout and walk up to the plate to bunt and make base hits. Who knows, you could even "win" the game you've always wanted to, just not the way you thought you would.

I believe it's worthwhile here to remind you of five key ideas.

THE MARKET IS EFFICIENT

No matter what information or insights you have, you can't gain a meaningful advantage over anybody else investing in the market. That's because whatever news you heard or insights you have, other investors have heard or thought about them, too. And the price has already been calculated with your new tip, along with all other relevant information baked in.

It hasn't always been this way. The passage of Rule 10b-5 of the SEC Act of 1934[25] made trading off insider informa-

---

25 Securities and Exchange Commission, *Securities Exchange Act of 1934*, https://www.govinfo.gov/content/pkg/COMPS-1885/pdf/COMPS-1885.pdf.

tion illegal (although the rule wasn't widely enforced until the 1970s). Until then, brokers were in a league of their own. They have always had access to a lot of information—and until recently, a lot of very valuable and inefficiently distributed information. By way of their position, they had personal relationships with the senior management of big public companies. Thus, the brokers had information about what these companies were doing, who was applying for patents on new ideas, and how businesses were growing. That same stockbroker, who did business with the top executives at the biggest companies, then had very wide latitude to take the information he learned and apply it to other client portfolios. This gave his clients a true and spectacular advantage in the marketplace.

Come 1968, the Supreme Court handed down a decision in the case of *SEC v. Texas Gulf Sulphur Co.* that marked the beginnings of strict enforcement of insider trading laws. This leveling of the playing field greatly reduced the impact a broker might have to influence any "super-informed" decision making.

Then consider the advent of the internet in the 1990s, which facilitates the spread of all information. Nowadays, everything we need to make a trade is in the palm of our hands. We have unlimited access to nearly all information and the space to develop our opinions. All ours, for free. The ground that was once so complicated and far off is now near. The "information advantage" has gone very flat since information gathering has become democratized and pedestrianized entirely. Yes, you can see that access is dangerous, as we've discussed already, but do you see what I mean? The market is efficient.

BOOMS AND BUSTS HAPPEN

Second, boom and bust cycles are natural parts of the economy. Just as fear and greed drive the economy's participants, the stock market reflects the same moods and motivations. Recessions and stock market swoons tend to go hand in hand. As with any storm, the clouds break, and the sun shines again. While often painful, these are actually healthy events. Like a windstorm that breaks out dead branches, culling in the marketplace makes room for new growth. Additionally, there would be no premium offered in return for long-term participants taking those risks without the periodic spankings that cause others to head for the hills.

THE MARKET GOES UP 81 PERCENT OF THE TIME

Third, the market goes up 81 percent of the time.[26] This is a trend we've seen over the last 42 years. Yes, past performance does not indicate future results, but there is something to be noted about this pleasant reality.

---

26 Based on the Vanguard S&P 500 Fund from 1976 to 2018.

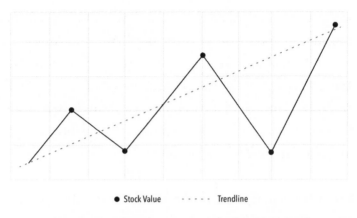

Stock Value   - - - - - Trendline

Large random market movements force stock prices above and below long-term trendline.
Replacement values of company assets ultimately support the lower bound of those core trends,
meaning aberrations above and below the trend will normally revert to that mean value over time.

An up-close look at each stock price ticking up and down multiple times per second makes the trajectory of the market or a single stock seem indefinable. To many investors, stock prices are just numbers on a page. Yet, if we break a "stock price" down into its base components, we see businesses and, ultimately, people. Here's why stocks go up so routinely: companies are made up of individual employees who want to do their jobs well, provide for their families, and gain personal fulfillment and betterment. Those people face losing their jobs if they don't perform their tasks efficiently and correctly. Sure, some companies will fail for various reasons, but for the marketplace as a whole, this natural incentive turns companies into results-generating machines that post positive profits over time.

The data prove this generally positive trend. In fact, looking at the Vanguard S&P 500 Fund, we found that from
any month in the past 42 years, the forward-looking one-
year return of the market was positive 81 percent of the
time. That doesn't mean that 81 percent of all years are
positive. It means that based on past results, there is an
81 percent chance that the forward one-year return from
any point in time will be positive.

From this same research we asked the question, "After
the market experiences a decline of 10 percent, how often
is the forward 365-day return positive?" The result is 91
percent. I know this to be true because the stock market
is run as an auction, and price equilibrium is determined
by the motivation and holding size of buyers and sellers.
The point when most people are considering getting out
of the stock market because "apparently everybody else
is doing so" is also when stocks are even more likely to
do well going forward. It's very counterintuitive, which
makes it hard to master for a human who survives on
intuition.

It's like sailing. I always thought that sailboats stayed
upright only because of a heavy keel that kept the boat
from rolling over. But in fact, as a boat tilts with the
wind, the laying over of the mast and sail nearer the
water releases most of the oppositional energy in the
wind. The angle of a side wind against a horizontal sail

is so shallow that the wind loses its pressure. That angle also exerts a maximum force on the keel trying to align itself under the boat. And so it is with the price of the stock market. The lower the prices go, the higher the mathematical pressure forcing them back upward. Emotional pressure has its own effect, too, but eventually, that always bows to the principle of reversion to the mean (the idea that the market will return to its average over time).

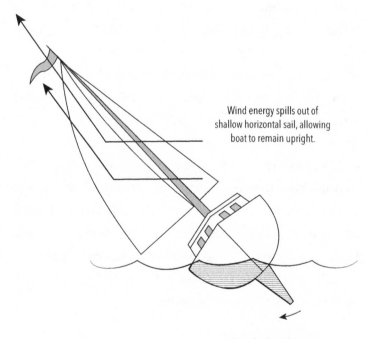

Wind energy spills out of shallow horizontal sail, allowing boat to remain upright.

Heavy keel weight wants to remain under boat.

STOCKS ARE CORRELATED

Fourth, the market is made up of stocks that, when put together in great numbers, increasingly move in the same direction as the market. This is called market correlation.

To put it simply, this means that as a group of securities moves up or down in price, other groups will follow in line very closely. Did you know that if you pick 10 stocks, and I pick another 10, our tiny lists are going to behave pretty similarly most of the time? But let's say you add in five more stocks, and I do the same. The correlation factor is going to go up, and our lists will behave even more similarly.

At around 40 or so names, several things start to happen. First, the odds are high that four stocks on your list and mine are identical since we both likely picked Microsoft, Apple, and a few others. The other 36 names average out most of the other peaks and valleys. Accordingly, the mutual funds that focus on big companies, where correlations are highest, will have a very difficult time jockeying for position on a performance list since so many of their holdings are the same and usually have similar weightings as well. Sometimes a tenth of a digit is all that separates the top of the list from the bottom.

A study in 2008 by Travis Sapp and Xuemin Yan[27] deter-

---

27   T. Sapp and X. Yan, "Security Concentration and Active Fund Management: Do Focused Funds Offer Superior Performance?" *The Financial Review* 43, no. 1 (2008): 27–49.

mined that the average mutual fund held 90 securities, but that 20 percent of all funds held 228 or more. What if you own 16 mutual funds? Pretty soon, it's not individual stock picking that matters but macro factors instead. Therefore, you can only achieve excess returns if you concentrate in just a few names. But that adds risk that most investors just simply won't tolerate when it goes against them, which it inevitably will. They normally choose to diversify into many stocks or many mutual funds to mitigate those concentration risks, and that's when other factors start to drive results.

FEES AND TAXES MATTER

Lastly, fees and taxes matter. Those who pursue excess performance will always boast about the potential for great gain without talking much about what you will surely lose in fees and taxes. These two primary factors conspire to drive performance below a market return because a market return is nearly void of both.

I talk about fees and taxes like a broken record. That's because people just have so little clue about how all this works. It's not their fault; it's just that the average individual investor is often in the dark about the true fee rate their accounts are charged and how the layers of costs add up. They rarely understand that fees can be stacked within their accounts. Sometimes there's a layer of fee from the firm and another from the products they put you in. There may also be a commission or markup in the stocks you purchase or a spread in the muni bonds they sold you.

Let me walk you through this. You might have a portfolio for which your advisor charges a 1 percent management fee and think, "Hey, that's not too bad." If it is filled with mutual funds and the like, charging their average expense ratio of 0.92 percent, you might think, "All right, just a small cost of playing the game." But add those together with the occasional 12b-1 fee, some turnover costs, and a potential sales load hidden within each product, and you've got a small math equation taking a large sum of your returns. In a year during which the assets in your portfolio return 5 percent, the fees reduce your return to somewhere around 3 percent, eating up 40 percent of your possible return and barely keeping pace with inflation. And in a year in which the assets return –1 percent... ouch. That's why it's important to think about fees as a percentage of *returns*, not a percentage of *account value*. This is one reason (among others to be discussed in the next chapter) to ensure your advisor's interests are aligned with yours because some might be profiting from more than one layer of those costs.

An even greater and remarkably misunderstood contributor to lagging performance is tax drag. Why is that? To start, taxes feel inevitable. People are used to the government wanting a share of all their profits but not so much their losses. But the average investor is ill-informed on how and when taxes are levied on their investments. So let's talk about that.

When an investor purchases a security, the amount they pay is termed cost basis. Over time, as the security rises or falls in value, the difference between the current or "market value" and the cost basis is called an unrealized gain or loss, and this amount changes as the price moves. At this time, the only taxes owed from this investment are those on the income it distributes. When the investor sells the security, the gain/loss morphs from unrealized to realized. As soon as it is realized, the gain becomes taxable.

Investment service providers typically hang their hats on a transactional methodology, which, as I just mentioned, is exactly what brings about taxes that erode compounded return. Some advisors don't plug this into their methodologies and fall back on clichés like "Taxes cannot be avoided, and they confirm you're making money." But the truth is that taxes are highly controllable and are avoidable altogether if you understand the tax code and what it allows and if you adapt your methodologies accordingly. Unfortunately, low tax drag is incompatible with most investment presentations, and far too few people ask the right questions.

Let's dig a little deeper. If a profitable security is held for less than 366 days before being sold, it is deemed to be a short-term realized gain and is taxed at the investor's ordinary income tax rate, a maximum rate of 39.8 percent. Investors with lower earned income and other factors might pay less. If the same security is held for 366 days or longer at a profit, it is called a long-term realized gain when sold, and taxes are capped lower. The rate is normally about half the ordinary income tax rate for each investor but is currently capped at 20 percent plus a 3.8 percent Medicare surtax, so 23.8 percent. Dividends paid out to investors are normally treated to this lower tax rate as well. The extra 15 percent (high 30s vs. low 20s tax rate) or so in taxes makes slower transactional methodologies a strong favorite and is yet another contributing factor to the downfall of trading systems that bounce around too much. Realized losses are deductible against realized gains. However, if net loss persists, those losses are generally not deductible against ordinary income (only other investment gains). There are two exceptions to this rule:

1. You can deduct losses against ordinary income in years in which realized losses exceed realized gain (but the limit is $3,000 per year).
2. The second exception is that net losses beyond that $3,000 can be carried over to future years (tax loss carryforward) and deducted indefinitely against future gains or the $3,000 annual income limit. It seems that's a pretty lopsided system favoring the govern-

ment. However, since the IRS also allows erasure of all unrealized gain at the owner's death, you do have a chance to even the playing field.

You can clearly see from that math how much of an advantage you could have if you adopted certain strategies. Foremost among them would be low trading turnover, which increases the odds of a tax-free step-up in basis at death and contributes to lower trading costs and lower management fees, offering multiple levels of additional compounding. Don't expect your broker to like this idea; any opposition you sense is a pretty clear indicator they might have agendas that run counter to your success.

THE STEP-UP IN BASIS RULE

In a morbid twist, the kindest gesture the IRS makes to every investor occurs at the time of their death. This "gesture" is one of the most powerful inter-generational asset accumulation strategies that exists. At the death of an investor, any gains you have accumulated over your lifetime (excluding those in your tax-deferred accounts) are forgiven. Your heirs will inherit any asset you owned, but the cost basis will be "stepped up" to the value on the date of your death.

Let's refer back to my client who bought $5,500 worth of Union Pacific stock back in 1974. His investment was worth $625,000 at his death in 2016, $619,500 of which was an unrealized gain. Had he sold that stock before he died, he would have paid nearly $250,000 in taxes. The Step-Up in Basis Rule wiped that tax liability out for his wife, meaning she inherited the whole $625,000 tax-free. And when his wife dies, their children will get to capitalize on this rule again to wipe away the taxes on any additional gain above the $625,000 of Union Pacific she received at her husband's death.

7 TIPS FOR BETTER INVESTMENT RESULTS

That's a lot of gab to say one thing: there's more at stake than meets the eye.

So how do you avoid paying these taxes and fees? We'll be diving into more of this in the next chapters, but before we do, I thought it'd be worthwhile to suggest a few tips that will take you back to facts, logic, and reason. This is no theory here, just the market at work. We need to cast aside the idea that self-serving prescriptions will get us what we want, when we want it, and instead think clearly about money and how we are to engage with it.

TIP #1 PROPERLY ASSESS RISK APPETITE.

Hands down, the most destructive mistake I see among investors is an inaccurate assessment of their true risk appetite. Most new investors have two opposing standards. One applies when things go well and another when things go badly. Many people talk a big game about how resilient they are but turn into crybabies when the winds shift.

Our client onboarding process includes a meeting at which I run the client through a bit of a gamut. I ask a series of questions that allow us to envision their mindset on profits and losses. The questions surround past market downturns, asking how they tolerated or responded to the shifting of the plates. Did you own stocks? Did you liquidate? What kind of an emotional roller coaster were you on? Do these patterns reflect the way your family handled money when you were growing up?

People will say, "Oh, I'm a long-term investor." But if we dig a little deeper, we find that oftentimes they actually mean, "I can handle many years of very *profitable* investing." They'll go on to declare, "I can endure downturns that are expected to occur in a market cycle." But what they actually mean is, "I think I have a pretty good grip on what the future holds, and if I happen to be wrong, I'll just dodge every bullet with my sheer agility." Bad idea. It's better to calibrate your level of loss aversion and tailor a portfolio to your personality and goals through *all* market environments, not just some. The importance of getting this right cannot be overstated.

This does not mean you assess your risk appetite only once. You have to regularly revisit the matter, keeping in mind that risk tolerance and goals shift depending on life stage and circumstances. When you're young and have many years of investing ahead of you, your risk tolerance is likely fairly high. You have time on your side to recover from anything the market throws your way. As you're nearing retirement, however, your goals and portfolio allocation might need to shift. Now that you have less time to recover from curveballs, the 80/20-equity-to-fixed-income risk profile of your youth may not fit anymore.

Some people wait until major market movements to find this out and end up making a mess of their investments and their psyche. Restructuring a portfolio during periods of rapid market movements is one of the most self-destructive actions an investor can take. If you discover in the midst of a 25 percent market decline that you can't stomach that kind of turmoil with your current portfolio allocation, restructuring at that time will guarantee you participate only in the downside, with no opportunity to recover. So be brutally honest with yourself here. Then, no matter how confident you are that you have it right, I recommend giving yourself some margin or "extra room," however you want to say it. Famed author and life coach Richard Swenson said, "Margin is the space between our load and our limits."

TIP #2 DECIDE TO BE A RESIDENT, NOT JUST A VISITOR.

An important distinction that marks successful investors is the ability to act as a resident of the marketplace, not just a visitor. People often get spooked by economic cycles and jump in and out of the market willy-nilly as the environment changes. They're like first-time snow skiers deciding the best way to get down is simply putting weight on one leg, then on the other, pausing occasionally trying to figure out which mogul is coming next and how to avoid it. Looking ahead, there are many opportunities to wipe out, which is confusing to the first-time skier who from his perch on the ski lift moments earlier thought it didn't look so bad. That's only because the farther away you get from the actual slope, the smoother it appears. When you fly over a ski slope, it just looks like a smooth blanket of snow.

With money, people tend to drill down into the minutiae, and they see it all as steep and bumpy, with terrifying moguls to be avoided. The problem is, that leads to perceiving the market as a place you only want to visit during times of "smooth sailing." It becomes a place you can only handle in small doses. So people go in and out, visiting with their money here and there, when the coast looks clear, only to try to back out before anything goes bad.

This has terrible repercussions, mostly in terms of fees, taxes, and opportunity costs. Most people have a wildly inaccurate perception of what bump is coming next and how to navigate it, but because we're gracious with ourselves in our evaluation of what actually happened, we do it all again and again and again. We totally misread how we've done, and we totally miss out on long-term compounding, swapping it for errors we could have avoided had we just left it all alone. What we really should do is build a customized portfolio like we would a home, become a resident, and ride it out.

TIP #3 ADOPT AN ABUNDANCE MENTALITY.

Adopting a worldview of abundance doesn't require accumulating layers of excess, but it does require a perspective that you have plenty. Even those with very little can perceive they have much, and much more they surely can have with that perspective.

It would be logical to believe that being protective of your money would lead to having more of it. In some cases, maybe so. But protectiveness closes many doors in investing and keeps profits from your pocket. The scarcity worldview leads to a stunted risk appetite, paltry annual returns, shifting strategies late in a trend, and larger and more frequent tax liabilities. The need to guard every penny leads to hoarding and the unceasing perception of being under attack.

It would also be logical to believe that being free with your money would lead to having less of it. In some cases, maybe so. But in investing, freedom opens many doors that can more than compensate for any short-term financial squeezes. The abundance mentality leads to a healthier risk appetite, the ability to make bolder moves earlier in the onset of a trend, and the confidence to do the hard thing when fear comes knocking at your door. Releasing your grip leads to a more reliable accumulation of long-term profits, rather than fueling the chasing of gains. Finally, greed can be nipped in the bud and you can have space to execute the proper strategy at the proper time.

Sounds great, doesn't it? How does one make this shift? I would argue that the key to this abundance mentality lies in your willingness to be generous with what you do have. I'm not pushing for wastefulness or frivolity—rather, the opposite. I think the process starts with gratitude and really seeing yourself as someone who has plenty. We'll dig deeper into this in the next chapter.

TIP #4 TAKE THE LONG-TERM PERSPECTIVE.

We can't talk about taking the long-term perspective in investing without talking about Warren Buffett, one of the most successful investors of all time. Although Buffett seems to enjoy the limelight, he's actually quite humble about his successes. Other stellar investors will claim their success is due to their extraordinary ability to feel market tremors and make the right move at the right time. On the other hand, Buffett will tell you to buy market exposure, be patient, and keep calm when the market fluctuates, knowing that it inevitably will. It's that simple.

When he attended Columbia University in 1950–51, Buffett was a student of the financial luminary Benjamin Graham. Buffett described Ben Graham's book *The Intelligent Investor* as "by far the best book on investing ever written." In this book, Graham uses an allegory of "Mr. Market" to show investors that the majority of the flurry in the stock market that occurs on a daily basis is simply noise and that they should be looking for investment opportunities based on value and price, not on emotion and timing. When Mr. Market, an extremely emotional man, tells you your holdings are suddenly worth 3 percent less today than they were yesterday, you shouldn't join him in a tizzy. Instead, you should consider the long-term perspective that more reasonably suggests you stay calm and stay put when Mr. Market is yelling, "Get out!"

With seven or so decades of investing under his belt, Warren has the wisdom and experience to see that we must use a wide-angle lens to get the long-term perspective. He said, "There's always gonna be some news, good or bad, every day. In fact, if you go back and read all the papers for the last 50 years, probably most of the headlines tend to be bad...But if you look at what happens to the economy, most of the things [that] happen are extremely good. I mean, it's incredible what will happen over time." I have fewer years as an investor under my belt, but I have found this perspective to be true. As the market tends to jump wildly up and down with each dramatic news headline, it reliably crawls upward as the economy grows.

TIP #5 SHIFT FROM SPECULATING TO INVESTING.

Most people's first experience with an investment is usually not an investment at all but a speculation.

I remember when I was in my young adult transition back in the '80s and thought it would be a great idea to buy a washateria for $10,000 and collect all those quarters, day in and day out...and then I realized how much work I'd be signing myself up for. What happened when a dryer broke or a washer flooded the store? So instead, I figured I would much rather invest in some stocks and make money with a lot less effort. I opened a brokerage account (before I became a broker myself) with a Dean Witter broker I met when I lived in New Orleans in 1983. This guy had given me the spiel on Continental Illinois National Bank and how it was on the road to bankruptcy but how he thought it was just about to rise from the ashes and become this spectacular investment. So I bought a few shares. Oh yeah, baby, I was going to hit the long ball. Well, that blew up in my face. Then I bought a little bit of this and a little bit of that to make up for my total loss in Continental Illinois. Boom! It blew up in my face again. All the while, I never really gave much thought to companies like Coca-Cola, which were just chugging along, buying small competitors, increasing in value, and distributing their 3 percent dividends.

The difference between a speculation and an investment really comes down to the attitude of the investor. If your goal is to generate income and long-term appreciation, that's an investment. If you're looking for a quick transaction with high risk and high reward, that's a speculation. Investments are conservative; speculations are aggressive. Investments are based on facts; speculations are based on ideas.

Sure, big, stable companies like Coca-Cola are boring compared to the thrill of startups and cryptocurrencies. But the likelihood of our picks going from $0.50 to $50 is pretty much zero. Often, people make speculations as I did, get burned, and eventually conclude that the stock market just isn't for them. They transition into real estate and the like. The thing is, though, they never made an investment to begin with. They were speculating, and those blow-ups gave them a warped perception of risk. They packed their bags and headed for greener pastures.

In reality, true investments have a much more docile future than a string of speculations and can yield fantastic results. It's a great idea to get invested with a company like Coca-Cola and stick with them for the long haul. Finding that early opportunity or insight into the next Amazon or Apple is awesome but often not highly impactful to a lifetime of investing. I have seen portfolios become a hundred times more valuable through patience, without ever owning a "magic stock."

TIP #6 GAIN CHEAP AND SIMPLE EXPOSURE AND LET IT SIT.

There's an old principle called Occam's razor, attributed to the fourteenth-century English theologian and philosopher named William of Occam, which states that the simplest solution is almost always the better solution. It draws upon the idea that at each juncture, we have an opportunity to make the wrong assumption, ultimately leading us to the wrong conclusion. Thus, he posited, the fewer junctures and assumptions, the better. This theory has applications in many fields of study, and it holds some truth in the investing world, too. When we overcomplicate things, we add uncertainty, which fuels our desire to react emotionally. Emotion then clouds our vision, leading to shortsighted decision making. This can make one's investment path full of unnecessary twists and turns, creating friction costs, taxes, and so forth.

The best way to simplify and minimize decision making in investing is a method called indexing. Indexing is a strategy that enables investors to diversify by mimicking the holdings in a broad index, such as the Dow Jones Industrial Index or the S&P 500, without making individual stock purchases. You can easily own hundreds or even thousands of companies by purchasing shares of an index fund that owns pools of companies, that might include Coca-Cola, Apple, Amazon, and in the case of an S&P 500 index fund, 497 other solid picks. Each company in the pool has its own individual weighting, and because there are often many different industries represented, a short-term disruption from a single company cannot impact the equilibrium. This method of gaining market exposure is very easy to achieve, thanks to the availability of mutual funds and ETFs, which mimic these indexes.

Index investing is the perfect vehicle to utilize with the powerful "pick and stick" methodology because it provides you with market exposure and, if you'll let it, protects you from the weight of failed decision making. For proof of the latter, you only have to look at the *SPIVA Report* (mentioned in Chapter 3) that perennially reveals indexes beat active managers 90 percent of the time. Indexing allows you to mentally check out because you can't feel each tremor miles below the surface, so you don't end up making tactical changes at the worst times. Indexing also requires less administration by the fund companies and thus can be very inexpensive for the investor. And because less of your money goes to management, this allows you to lock in near market-matching returns, year after year. Don't forget that market-matching returns are nothing to sneeze at, as the market earns an average 8 percent return annually. The math of compounding that rate of return over time will blow your mind.

Growth of $1 Million Investment over 50 Years

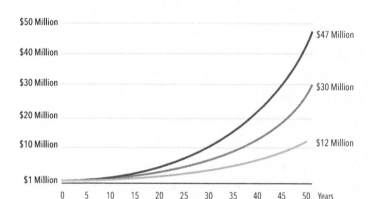

Small changes made to retain tax advantages and cut management costs can have profound effects over time. For a $1 million investment over 50 years, the seemingly small difference between a 7% and 8% rate of return would result in a difference of $17 million.

If you need emotional reassurance from your ability to play the market, this is not your route. But if you want to make the most money, after fees and after taxes, the pick-and-stick methodology is the most efficient way to construct your portfolio.

TIP #7 DON'T GIVE IN TO GREED.

Momentum is a very sexy thing, but chasing it can be a fool's errand. Look at America Online (AOL), which was trading at $16 a share in early 1998. By mid-'98, it was $23 a share, and people were scared it was going to fall. Then in late '99, it was $500 a share. And then people got greedy, thinking, *Oh my gosh, I can make so much money! And fast! Maybe I should buy some more.* They thought the sky was the limit! AOL would go to a thousand bucks! They were more convinced than ever it was going to go up. Then came the dot-com bust. It went back down to $125.

Although getting rich quickly sounds ideal, that line of thinking undermines a proper perspective. Greed hijacks discipline, muddles long-term investment plans, and leads people to make the emotional decisions we've talked so much about.

I remember watching Daffy Duck cartoons when I was a kid. The recurring theme was that Daffy always got into trouble while trying to get "Rich, Rich, Rich!" I've seen this same energy course through people's veins as they talk through their hopes to scratch the itch of greed; they'll play the lottery, buy penny stocks, chase stock tips, or buy mating emu pairs, tulips, and bitcoin. Dollar signs in the eyes can also lead people to cut corners, cut relationships, mar reputations, and all kinds of other foul balls.

This is a much deeper issue, but often the solution to this predisposition is for one to take a step back and say, "Look, an 8 percent average return is good enough for me." (Especially if I can get a portion of it as cash flow and not have the government participating in my earnings.) The math on an 8 percent compounded annual rate of return, with no fees or taxes over a lifetime...again, it's enough to make your head explode. But some people want to shoot for 1,000 percent returns. It may feel good, but it's much more likely to blow up in your face and in more ways than one.

I started this chapter with a quote from a friend of mine, Ross Kyger. It reads, "Knowledge comes from experience, but wisdom, that's the good stuff. And wisdom comes from bad experience." And really, this puts the cap on every other tip I just gave.

The market deals hands that we could never anticipate in advance. And while so many people will tell you otherwise, there are a million different ways to mess up. If and when this happens to you, you will have to learn from your mistakes. That's how you learn to go a better way.

CHAPTER SIX

CHOOSE DIFFERENTLY

"An abundance mentality springs from internal security, not from external rankings, comparisons, opinions, possessions, or associations."

—STEPHEN COVEY, AUTHOR OF *THE 7 HABITS OF HIGHLY EFFECTIVE PEOPLE*

I often picture my clients in one big room with an aisle down the middle, almost like a church. On the left side, we have the relaxed, easy-to-deal-with, high-performing portfolio clients. And on the right side, we have the uptight folks, clients who always call to ask questions about the market, always wondering if they should buy or sell their holdings, and whose portfolios consistently lag behind. A few people float the room a bit, but most are either clinging to the left wall or to the right wall.

I used to sit back and wonder what caused people to be on the left or on the right. Was it ambivalence? Were the folks on the left side just not that concerned with their money? Were the ones on the right just so meticulous that they had to ensure they weren't about to get slammed? Or were they simply entertained by it all?

And then it dawned on me. It wasn't ambivalence.

It all came together for me when I was visiting a church in Fort Worth in 2018. The guest pastor, Ben Stuart, was talking about relationships. He said, "When you have a source of life, you are a source of life. But where there is scarcity, desperation sets in. And desperation leads to exploitation of others." The same applies to our money. When we believe our needs will be met, we are generous with our resources. We become a source of life to those around us. We have an abundance mentality. But when we always live in fear of running out, wondering when the roof is going to cave in, we look for threats to our sense of security. This mentality leads us to find boogeymen behind every bush. The weariness from the discomfort leads to overreaction and it all becomes fatiguing. That's the scarcity mentality.

An abundance mentality can also impact your perspective on charitable giving. I find that generous givers also tend to be the best risk takers. You might assume this has to do with the ability to give, but I assure you, it's more than that. It has much more to do with one's relationship with one's money. If that relationship is unhealthy, they'll hoard it and hope that no one comes knocking. But if one can decide to come out from under the veil of hoarding and begin to give more freely, they will almost immediately break the bonds of the scarcity mindset. As with the chicken-and-egg question, I'm unsure which part comes first. Did giving freely break the bondage? Or was the bondage broken first, allowing the freedom? I cannot speak to the order in which this occurs, but I can speak with certainty that the connection exists. I want to challenge you to think deeply about this.

TOOLS FOR GIVING

Did you know you can give appreciated stocks to charities? Rather than write a $5,000 check to your favorite charity, you can donate stock worth $5,000 instead. The embedded gain is not taxable to any 501(c)(3), allowing you to wash your hands of the taxes you would otherwise owe on your long-term capital gains and simultaneously support your favorite charity. You can then use the $5,000 cash you saved to reinvest for yourself (you could even buy the same stock again).

My favorite charitable giving tool is a donor-advised fund. When we take ownership of our resources too seriously and hoard them, per our nature, then every request from a charity seems an affront to our personal sense of security. But if we decide to hold our resources more loosely, then establishing an account with a donor-advised fund is a must.

With a donor-advised fund, we essentially get a "locker" from which we can distribute gifts to charities at any time. Once money is deposited into the fund, we can no longer retrieve it, releasing us from the emotional toll of giving. The money is already "gone." However, we can decide which of our favorite charities receives the money. Since the fund operates like a charity itself, our irretrievable deposits count as charitable gifts and are tax deductible when the deposit is made into the fund (not when we decide to push it to a specific charity).

This can also help streamline the process for large gifts that we wish to allocate out later in smaller doses, such as large stock gifts. Typically, stock gifts are complicated and cumbersome, and you want to make them as infrequently as possible while still retaining the tax benefits. So it's best to make a one-time donation into a donor-advised fund, receive the tax benefits, then distribute the money from the fund in doses.

The donor-advised method of giving can be super practical, but it can be even more powerful in breaking the emotional bonds we have to our resources. It makes it easier to be generous when charities later make their requests because the money we've set aside is not ours anymore anyway. Mechanized giving makes our demons seem more like paper tigers.

MY TALE OF TWO PATHS

If you've kept up with my musings (blog address: www.seg-mentwm.com/blog) over the years, you might recognize these names and remember this story. But some stories are worth telling again and again.

Two of my clients died in 2017. We'll call them Barry and Alvin. I had worked with both of them for more than a decade before I learned that they had gone to college together 60 years before, some 2,000 miles away. As it turns out, they were born in the same year, graduated in the same year, married in the same year, and as I mentioned, died in the same year. They both retired in 1994 and lived off their nearly identical $3.5 million nest eggs during their 23 years of retirement. But as profound as their similarities were, their investing styles were polar opposites, as were their results.

Barry was fidgety and insecure, and Alvin was patient and optimistic. Barry would watch his money online every day and squeal with each nasty market drop, wondering each time if the sky was falling. Alvin barely noticed, and if he did, he was scanning his cash to buy more stocks at every drop.

As time went on, Alvin's portfolio value rose steadily, and his dividend earnings (yield) escalated as company stock dividends increased and increased again. Conversely, Barry's income was derived mostly from interest, since bonds fit better with his low tolerance for market swings. This limited Barry's income potential. It also caused greater taxes than Alvin paid on dividend income because bond interest is taxable as ordinary income (as high as 39.8 percent), and taxes on stock dividends are capped at 23.8 percent.

Barry would only venture periodically into stocks, whenever he thought "the coast was clear." These moves seemed to be connected to many months of significant gains in the market, which left him with FOMO (fear of missing out). This lousy timing put Barry directly in harm's way, having invested only after stocks had a great run.

Accordingly, Barry's portfolio was relegated to never gaining value because bonds mature in the future at their value today and because Barry would only hold a stock if it was at a profit and proceed to sell it whenever his whims said it turned negative. You can see how Barry ended up in the certainty of bonds.

I often talked to Alvin about certainty, risks, stocks, bonds, and stability because I loved the way he thought. He always replied, "Why would I ever own bonds? Stocks always bounce back. As long as my dividends get paid, what does the current share price matter to me? Certainty is overrated." Now, that's Warren Buffett language. Preach it, Alvin!

Barry, on the other hand, needed assurance of the present

state of his investment. At each market decline, the talking heads on TV prompted emotional responses, and Barry was always quick to run for cover, despite my admonishment. Worse, he did his most significant damage in ways I could not see in a side trading account. After Barry died, his CPA surprised me with news that he had racked up $400,000 in tax-loss carry forward from trades in that side account. Barry left his widow $3.5 million, the same amount he had at his retirement 23 years earlier...well, sort of. Inflation had actually cut the value of that original amount in half, and unfortunately, he also left his kids a $1 million tax liability because he owned an annuity in his pension (and a big IRA that his wife will have to pay only part of the income taxes on, meaning the kids will get hit later).

Meanwhile, Alvin's retirement nest egg of $3.5 million in stocks became $19 million by the time he passed. He never even reinvested any dividends, meaning he withdrew all earned cash and let only profits pile up.

Alvin's situation is the poster child for the power of the Step-Up in Basis Rule. Alvin's widow received all assets in taxable accounts free and clear of any capital gains tax. Of that wealth, $7.5 million was legally an untaxed gain since he carried many stocks on his books for over 30 years without any sales. The kids will also receive another cleansing of capital gains taxes when their mother passes due to the same tax rules.

That's the power of the Step-Up in Basis Rule: Alvin's kids will likely owe zero taxes despite inheriting six times as much value as Barry's kids. Do you see the striking contrast between these two men?

Barry and Alvin both had fantastic personal attributes. They simply had different perspectives on the future, likely emanating from how they were raised and the risks and opportunities that were burned into their psyches. I would bet a small fortune that Barry had experienced some financial trauma early in life that he vowed never to repeat. On the other hand, I know for a fact Alvin had endured his own share of financial trauma but somehow was able to become an eternal optimist and his actions reinforced his faith in the future. Alvin always perceived the future as bright, and Barry always perceived it as ominous.

There's an ancient method of capturing monkeys called the South Indian monkey trap. The trap is built out of a hollowed-out portion of a tree with just enough space for a monkey to get his folded hand in but small enough that the monkey's hand will be stuck when full of bait and clenched into a fist. As long as the monkey refuses to let the food go, the monkey is trapped. The idea that he's found his bounty for the day holds him captive. Now all the hunter has to do is come and collect the monkey who, by his own choice, is stuck. Some find this surprising since monkeys are pretty smart and would probably be savvy enough to let it go. But was Barry?

More importantly, are you?

Barry was trapped by an idea, unable to see that the principles that caused him to hold so tightly to his money had become lethal. Sure, he ended up with the certainty that his $3.5 million would stay his $3.5 million, but I can tell you, he lost much in his hours of worry, strain, relational toil, and in the end, the opportunity to earn at least market-matching returns which would have led to far more monetary success.

The reality is, Barry learned to clench his fist with every ebb and flow. Fearing change, regret, and loss of any kind, he would hold on to every cent he could, trying to squeeze two pennies out of one. He was so rigidly attached to his ideas of what would lead to his freedom that he ended up with mediocre semi-confinement at best. But Alvin... somewhere along his way, Alvin's mindset shifted gears, and I'm hoping yours will, too.

DEAR JOHN

Every couple of months, a client refers me to one of their friends. Typically, we are introduced via email and decide to meet up for a good cup of gumbo and talk about family history and investment experience. This tends to give me plenty of perspective to work with, and the same profiling occurs on their end. The conversation eventually leads to how they arrived at this spot. Almost every time, they have had their share of bad experiences and are looking for an advocate who knows the system. By the end of our lunch, I can surely tell if they have an abundance or scarcity mentality and whether we'd be a good fit for working together. To be perfectly frank, I have let quite a few otherwise "ideal" clients pass by if I discern their relationship with their money would preclude any real success for them. It's just not worth the headaches to take on a client with a tight grip on money and a loose grip on perspective. Oftentimes, these prospects ring the "Barry" bells, and I end up sending them an email like this one:

Dear John,

I've been thinking about our conversation and have concluded that you may need a coach more than an investment advisor. Based on our conversation and how eager you seem to get a good handle on your money, I'm guessing you would appreciate some candor, as you may have never received it since people in my position often go for appeasement rather than constructive criticism.

Over my years in the business, I've noticed a pattern among many high-net-worth individuals. Somewhere along their way, they experienced some type of financial trauma and made up their mind they would never go back there again. For some, it could have been a family bankruptcy, and for others, it may have been the 2008 meltdown. In any case, I believe this leads to an unhealthy relationship with money, most notably the tendency to see money as a way to keep score. Scorekeeping can create an unhealthy aversion to risk and consequently lead to pretty big mistakes. Surely, this is only conjecture on my part, but I think we'd both like to see something different for you.

Although you have tremendous knowledge of the markets and their intricacies, many of your possible returns have been lost to "overthinking it." At some point, we have to acknowledge that proper perspective is as important, if not more important, than understanding.

That being said, going it alone may prove to be low cost, but the cost of not fully participating is multiples worse for you. You might just need an accountability partner who knows the game, too.

I have my own demons that I battle, and I don't stand in judgment. I only offer my observations that come from my experience in hopes that you can become a better investor for it. Holding on a little looser would be an excellent start for us both.

Gil

Some reply to these letters, and some don't. But the ones who do are often grateful for the honesty. Yet there are habits, patterns, and ways of doing things that they just have the hardest time getting away from. It's pretty awesome when I see people beat back their demons. I've seen people change, and I mean really change.

PEOPLE CHANGE

I could tell you many stories about my clients' victories, but if you look back on my own story, which I shared in Chapter 2, you'll see that this kind of "Dear John" letter very well could have been written to me. In fact, I wish it had been. My own financial trauma from my childhood fueled my pursuit of success. I wanted to do well for myself. I wanted "the good life." More than that, I wanted the freedom that seemed to come from having a ton of money.

By the time I was 40, I had my wife and three kids relying on me. I started to feel the pressure to provide for them with greater intensity. You know how it goes...mortgage, college, and so on; I just didn't feel like I had enough wiggle room. Although I was well into my career in financial services, I still couldn't totally see the patterns of the way the market ebbs and flows. I spent years and years trying to figure out my "angle" on the market, but I didn't understand the efficiency of the market, how the market ticks upward 81 percent of the time, nor the full implications of taxes and the like. So I put about 50 percent of my net worth into municipal bonds to keep my risk lower, and at the end of the day, I kept banging my head against the wall because I knew I was missing something.

Around that same time, my wife and I ran into an old friend of ours who always loved to talk about my clothes. He'd always say, "Oh man, that's a great suit you got on, Gil" or "Check out those shoes!" That night, he said, "Wow, I wish I had a tie like that!" I thanked him for the compliment and inexplicably felt compelled to take it off and give it to him. It wasn't a big gesture, but I knew he didn't have a nice tie rack like the one I had in my closet back home.

I went back to work the following Monday and couldn't stop thinking about the look on his face nor the freedom I felt after giving away what was actually one of my favorite ties. That same day, around lunchtime, my wife called to tell me about a fundraiser for an inner-city ministry here in Houston. I wasn't sure what was happening in me, but I felt the same compulsion to give, without pause, and without crunching the numbers.

Little did I know, I was slowly adopting the abundance mentality. It wasn't complicated; I just realized that even after giving away a tie and donating my money, I still had plenty. Over time, that mentality further colored my vision and changed the way I invested. Loosening my grip led to a healthier risk appetite which led to greater investment successes. More than that, it released me from my emotional aversion to my net worth dropping below my high-water mark.

I'm not proposing a karmic financial strategy that says if you give, you get. My experiences and observations only show the connection between having a loose grip on your money and the success you can achieve when you are free to let it work for you. Some say this is unnatural and impossible, but it's just a matter of willingness to embrace the challenge. I still have my demons that come knocking at my door, threatening the framework I've built over the years. Yet, every time I hear them, I know the choice is mine.

CHAPTER SEVEN

THE ADVISOR ADVANTAGE

"An advisor's most valuable role is to keep an investor in their seat."

—JOHN BOGLE, LEGENDARY INVESTOR, FOUNDER
AND CHIEF EXECUTIVE OF THE VANGUARD GROUP

One question people rarely ask me but surely must ask themselves is, "Should I even hire an advisor?" The reality is, you could choose not to. But I would argue that the benefit of having someone in your corner who has the roadmap, understands the terrain, and is looking out for your good is extremely valuable. You simply have to weigh those benefits against the cost. Traditional brokerage firm advice is even more expensive when you consider the fact that many traditional investment recommendations (such as actively managed mutual funds) significantly subtract from the investment return equation because of high fees and tax drag. I'm hopeful that this book has exposed those excess costs and how harmful they are and that you are now more inclined to hire a cost-sensitive advisor. You now have the ability to discern fact from fiction, leaving you to pay for only the most valuable offering in the financial services world: the relationship.

When going it alone, people take certain responsibilities upon themselves they might not be prepared for. It's like hiring a fishing guide who not only provides knowledge but a well-serviced boat full of fuel, ice, and backup gear in case you snarl your bait caster on the first throw. The guide won't be perfect, but they'll surely be helpful. They even have a cellphone full of other guides' numbers who can give tips if they find themselves lacking—greatly increasing the odds of finding fish and decreasing the risks that come with being out on the water.

Similarly, the unadvised investor takes on an incredible amount of responsibility. Yet, our selective memories (which are gentle with our egos), inadequate ability to interpret the tax code, insufficient understanding of the ways costs get allocated and layered, and our blindness to the time value of money virtually assure a mistake is forthcoming.

People struggle to interpret new information; they're iffy on the proper way to execute strategy. Not only that, but people who manage their own money have all kinds of emotional baggage from having too much at stake, too much perceived control over the outcome, too many past failures, and all kinds of creative ways to justify their poor choices to themselves.

The damage the unadvised investor inflicts upon themselves is addressed in a study published annually by the investment research firm DALBAR, called *Quantitative Analysis of Investor Behavior (QAIB)*. The study proves, year after year, that investor performance in mutual fund ownership lags the performance of the funds they buy. This is due to the timing of the inflows and outflows (purchases and sales made by investors), which are directly tied to investor sentiment about the future of the fund. The report cuts down on the noise about other factors that affect returns such as fees and taxes and strictly looks at how good investors are at deciding *when* to buy and sell. As it turns out, they're pretty awful at it; their poor timing routinely lops a third off the return that the mutual fund experienced.[28] That's because investors are performance chasing and self-protective. Their experience is a lot like a game of Whac-A-Mole but with money at stake.

Often, investors all lose their heads at the same time. In

28 Frank Armstrong III, "Just a Little Too Cute for Their Own Good," *Forbes*, August 16, 2019, https://www.forbes.com/sites/frankarmstrong/2019/08/16/just-a-little-too-cute-for-their-own-good/.

the midst of a frenzy, it's natural to think clear weather will never return, and in the midst of the calm, it's natural to think the seas will never get choppy. Both are wrong. As a matter of fact, the final crescendo of the selloff on March 23, 2020, amid the COVID-19 crisis, sparked a buying frenzy the next day that drove the Dow Jones Industrial Average (DJIA) up more than 15 percent, or 3,000 points in just 31 hours.[29] Sellers participated in all the downside and gave away their chance at a swift recovery.

A recent Bank of America study[30] showed that over the past nine decades, the 10 best days in each decade totally defined market returns. These 90 days were so important over the past 90 years that if you missed those, the remaining 89 years and nine months produced an aggregate market return of just 91 percent—not even a doubling of your money over 90 years. With those 90 days included, the aggregate market return was over 14,600 percent! The best days are almost always nestled up against days with horrific declines, so there's no advance notice when a good day is coming, and that's why emotional investors get scalped. March 24th and 25th of 2020 will surely make the list of the 90 most important investment days of the twenty-first century.

---

29 Reuters Eikon Database

30 Ben Winck, "Bank of America Reveals a Shocking Stat Showing Why Traders Should Stay Invested during Tough Times—or Risk Missing Out on Massive Gains," Business Insider, 2020, https://markets.businessinsider.com/news/stocks/stock-market-strategy-timing-long-positions-coronavirus-volatility-biggest-gains-2020-8-1029544867.

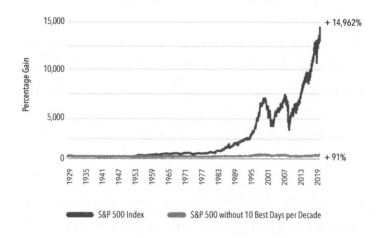

Impact of the Best 90 Days over the Last 90 Years

S&P 500 Index   S&P 500 without 10 Best Days per Decade

That's really where an advisor comes in. Their job is to save you from yourself. A proper advisor will coach you off the ledge and make you stick to your knitting when the going gets tough. They are built-in accountability, keeping you out of trouble. They are a delegated repository for your angst, keeping you from acting on the incessant threats. They watch out for the fine print and keep you from falling into fee and tax traps. An advisor can serve as an intermediary for couples who have opposing mindsets on risk and reward, and they can provide continuity, an advice bridge for clients who die unexpectedly. Above all, they are the ones responsible for thinking about what you should do next, and doing so impartially and in your best interest.

All that said, sourcing financial advice is a puzzle people

struggle to piece together. Many feel a lot of pressure to get it right, while simultaneously bearing the weight of the fact that they don't understand all the pieces in play. With so much potential for both success and failure, many feel paralyzed, while others are eager to get in on the action. In either case, traversing the financial advice landscape is difficult, and sooner or later, every investor will ask the question, "Who can help me with this?"

As we discussed, Wall Street is full of really smart people who make their living on investors navigating this process. Some are just name-brand salesmen in fancy suits looking for the next transaction, willing to pitch you on how their methodology will unlock the complexity and make you "rich, rich, rich!" Investors need to be ready to filter these offerings so they don't end up paying for services that are foolhardy to the core. How do you do that? The key is to know what you really want and what tools you'll need along the way.

PEOPLE WANT PEACE OF MIND

Everybody wants a good return: there's an allure to beating the S&P. But at the end of the day, what people want is peace of mind.

During my time at the brokerage firms, it was customary to periodically send out a questionnaire to clients asking them about the services we provided that they valued most. The questions focused on qualitative things such as how fast the advisor returned calls and quantitative things such as producing high returns. The results were always the same: clients valued the qualitative over the quantitative. They consistently ranked their priorities in this order: dealing with my problems, returning my calls, attending to my needs quickly, caring for my set of circumstances, and so forth. Performance rarely ranked in the top half of the clients' priorities. I think clients eventually realize they just might be their own worst enemy, and so they want a comrade, they want accountability, they want the peace of mind that comes from not going it alone.

The thing is, though, you should not go out and hire just any advisor.

A few months ago, my wife sent me to the store to get some tequila for these margaritas she loves to make. As I walked out the door, she said, "Get the George Clooney one! It's the best." So I tracked down handsome George's tequila, called Casamigos. I was amazed to find out it was three times as expensive as the stuff we normally buy, even though 100 percent agave tequilas are all very much the same. I thought that markup was ridiculous, and I bristled at the celebrity marketing. *How much better could George's tequila be?* I thought.

Particularly in the consumer space, many manufacturers sell exactly the same product in different packages to take advantage of our biases. So knowing that celebrity-branded products tend to offer nothing but fancier packages and higher prices, I decided to do an experiment. I brought both tequilas home and did a blind taste test with my wife to see which she thought was better. We then made margaritas with both types, according to her "skinny" recipe. And in each case, what did she choose? The one we always buy. Not George Clooney's. She actually likes the cheaper one more and legitimately thinks it's better, but somehow George Clooney is so good looking he makes average tequila seem otherworldly! It wasn't the tequila after all; it was the branding. The illusion of "I'm with him" can cost you a pretty penny. At the end of the day, it's just not worth it.

This also happens when trying to find "expertise" in the financial advice business. Going with the name brand can appease people's desire to be in on the game. I get it—it's sexy. You also see this prevalently in the orthopedic surgery game. Did you know that some doctors will pay professional sports teams to be known as the team physician? That's because the doctor gets a career advance that's more valuable than the team services he or she provides. Everybody wants to be able to tell their friends that their doctor is the team physician for the Houston Rockets. It has a valuable cachet. You also see this with former employees of Goldman Sachs. If you ever talk business with someone who has worked at Goldman, you might notice that fact tends to come up early in your conversation. I know a broker who was just a summer intern at Goldman and was not offered permanent employment thereafter. Despite that, he has spent a lifetime telling everyone he "used to work at Goldman Sachs." It's panache at work. Don't get me wrong, Goldman is a fine firm, possibly the best of the brokerage firms.

Unfortunately, many big-name brokerage firm brokers are about as good at identifying optimal investment vehicles as my wife is at identifying which tequila is worth $60. My point is that many individual investors want to link up with whoever appears to be the smartest guy in the room and let him tell them what to do and when. But the reality is, that's often not the best approach for clients. The hunt for the "smartest guy" can lead to great disappointment. What you should seek instead is a financial advisor you trust, who is interested in your problems, deals with them promptly, and provides you with proportionate performance for the risk that you're willing to take.

CUSTODY

The actual holder of your securities in the brokerage world is called your custodian. (Maybe that's because they clean up and make things orderly behind us.) Some think that switching over to an independent advisor means losing the backing of substantial and reliable firms. False. Brokerage firms like Charles Schwab and Fidelity provide secure and reliable (and cheap) storage places. You are still relying on the advisor for their prudence, judgment, and personalized advice, but the necessary brokerage machinations still exist. This separation of contracted services makes for a much less confined and conflicted ecosystem like you would find at a JP Morgan or Merrill Lynch.

MUDDLED MESS

How is it that investors so often miss this and hire financial advisors who continually overpromise and underdeliver? To start, investors are often confused by designations and for good reason. As I've mentioned, the sheer number of advisory-sounding titles and companies is enough to make your head spin. So to help clarify this mess, we'll specifically address the three components of an advisory relationship that every investor needs to understand: designations, registrations, and compensation.

DESIGNATIONS

In the investment advice world, there are many different titles that sound fairly similar but reveal important differences in the services provided. There are certified financial planners (CFPs) for the aspiring wealthy, estate planners (most often JDs) for the already wealthy, tax advisors or certified public accountants (CPAs) for folks who want to minimize tax impact, and "financial advisors" (portfolio managers, investment managers, asset managers, wealth managers, and brokers) for those who want guidance in investing their assets. What adds to the confusion is that many firms bundle multiple services into one. Investors *could* benefit from all these services, but I would contend that financial planning services aren't of primary concern to the very wealthy nor is estate planning an urgent need for those in accumulation mode. For the sake of the remainder of this conversation about financial services, we're going to limit our scope to those who might refer to themselves as "financial advisors." To choose well among all the advisory services, you must first understand the nature of the relationship you might have with each, much of which is determined by their registration obligations and compensation structures.

REGISTRATIONS

In the United States, anyone who offers official financial advisory services is required to be registered with a regulator. These regulators, as I've mentioned, are the Financial Industry Regulatory Authority (FINRA) and the Securities and Exchange Commission (SEC). FINRA is the largest independent regulator for all securities firms doing business in the United States, whereas the SEC is a government agency acting as the ultimate regulator of the securities industry. The SEC also oversees FINRA.

Financial advisors, investment managers, portfolio managers, asset managers, and wealth managers don't necessarily have to be registered with FINRA. In fact, registration directly with the SEC, and not FINRA, is what creates the "fiduciary distinction." SEC oversight, and the fiduciary distinction, requires advisors to act in the client's best interest, whereas FINRA oversight allows more freedom for brokers to choose suboptimal investments and doing only what is merely "suitable" for clients. We've discussed at length the ways the suitability requirement causes problems for investors, but I also acknowledge the reality that conflicted advice is better than no advice at all. The question every investor must consider when it comes to their relationship with their advisor is this: are their interests aligned with yours? Answering this question gives the investor valuable insight, making them better equipped to calibrate their dynamic with their advisor. And the easiest way to find the answer to that question is to follow the money.

COMPENSATION

As I said, brokers can (and do) refer to themselves as "advisors," befuddling investors on their relationship to the broker and how they're paying for the services they're receiving. The distinction that must be made here is that *nonfiduciary advisors (brokers) and fiduciary advisors are different*, and we can see this in the way they are paid.

Many brokers have a transactional relationship with their clients, whereby most interactions involve a "sales pitch." A true fiduciary advisor, however, provides ongoing, regular advice regarding total portfolio management and most often has the authority to make investment changes unilaterally, having what is called in the industry "discretionary authority". Brokers are compensated by commission for each transaction, sometimes based on which products they place their clients in and calculated with the dollar amount deployed. This requires prior approval on the part of the client because no representation is being made that those choices are surely best. Fiduciary advisors, on the other hand, are compensated based on the value of account under management (AUM), or hard-dollar fees, but in no way can that pay be connected to transactional activity. Because the fiduciary standard of care *requires* advisors to advocate for their clients' best interests, fiduciary advisors must charge a fee for their services and cannot earn commissions from the advice they give out. Ever.

An investor might have both commissionable accounts and fee-bearing accounts in their household, but each account number cannot have exposure to both fees and commissions. And so, compensation structure is assigned at the account level.[31] A nonfiduciary advisor

---

31   An account held at a brokerage or bank that has separate accounting and reporting by that account number. This allows brokerage firms to segregate their fiduciary and nonfiduciary business and follow regulatory rules on where they have conflicts of interest and how they must be disclosed to clients.

(FINRA-registered broker) can earn revenue through both channels: commissions *and* fees. Fiduciary status would mean your advisor generates revenue only through the fees that are shown as a line item on your statement. No obfuscation there. Fiduciaries are registered with the SEC and are not subject to FINRA's rules. Although you may occasionally get nearly identical advice from a commissioned advisor, the costs will likely be higher and more conflicted. It's easy to get confused when your broker talks about his fee-only accounts having fiduciary components, but you can see why a broker would focus on discussing that occasional alignment of interests with clients and his firm's fiduciary status as an advantage, leaving you with the impression that it's the norm across all of his accounts. Not only is it not the norm, but most brokers would also have to self-immolate to get it to be so.

To help you grasp the confusion that might arise in a relationship with a nonfiduciary advisor, imagine that you have four accounts at a big brokerage firm, two of which are commissionable and two of which are fee based. Your nonfiduciary advisor (broker) manages all four accounts, and while discussing your portfolio as a whole with you, he switches between his fiduciary hat and his nonfiduciary hat with ease. The distinction between his roles becomes blurry. He may have no intention to confuse, but even when your nonfiduciary advisor (broker) is honest, the confusion pollutes the relationship enough to prevent you from receiving truly fiduciary advice.

A broker who has discretionary power in one account *and* earns commissions on trading activity in another is faced with glaring conflicts. Many brokers in this position struggle to use their moral compass to navigate, which has led to huge problems in the brokerage world and meaningful legal settlements. Lots of brokers just cannot resist paying themselves to act. And you better believe Reg BI (laid out in Chapter 3) will prompt a rise in brokers claiming to be held to the fiduciary standard, even though compliance with the new regulation clearly does not bestow fiduciary status.

"WILL YOU ACCEPT FULL FIDUCIARY RESPONSIBILITY?"

There are a few easy ways to clear up this murky water. When your advisor tells you things like he's "practically a fiduciary" because of how honorably he manages your money, just calmly ask him to prove it. If he says he can, tell him you'd like a letter on company letterhead accepting full fiduciary responsibility in your relationship. If he's a true fiduciary, he will be happy to accommodate the request. If not, he will backpedal, revealing he's just a broker with big talk.

Another easy test is to ask if the advisor receives any 12b-1 revenue from mutual funds (remember, a 12b-1 is a kickback, plain and simple). No fully fiduciary advisor can accept 12b-1s. This will nip all that fiduciary talk in the bud and separate the wheat from the chaff very quickly.

WHAT DO PEOPLE NEED? ADVOCACY

Investors need an advocate, and the best way to get one in this business is to hire a fiduciary advisor. It's just like a game of block-and-tackle out there. People want to know someone is covering their blind side and looking out for their best interests. As they make progress, they want someone out front and following behind, blocking and tackling. That's precisely what we fiduciary advisors do.

While politicians grandstand about how they "look out for the little guy," much of what they do panders to the special interest groups that pay them (or their campaigns). Brokerage firms proudly talk about the small fragments of their business that are truly fiduciary but then pay lobbyists to seek legislative relief from being forced into a fiduciary role. That's because they want the issue obfuscated. The suitability standard of care, which is the touchstone of all FINRA-registered firms, causes your advisor to develop behavioral biases and give advice with certain slants. Some advisors can navigate these choppy waters honorably. But even the most honorable cannot escape the nasty machinations behind Oz's curtain.

Let me be clear, I'm not bad-mouthing commissionable and conflicted advice. Under some circumstances, it's the most efficient solution. Let's face some facts. You will not find an experienced fiduciary advocate to help unwind

Grandpa's hundred-thousand-dollar estate. It's too much work and too much legal responsibility for their cost structure. Paying commissions to a broker for a burst of time and services would be the most efficient arrangement. So there is surely a place for commissionable advice; it's just not the best option for those looking for a long-term advocacy relationship.

There's no question you're going to get more unbiased advice from any fiduciary advisor since their business model does not allow any double-dipping of clients. Many people would argue that those costs to clients still exist in the fiduciary world but that fiduciary advisors just don't get compensated for them. Nope. Fiduciaries know where those costs reside and have a duty to help clients avoid them. It's just like how Waze monitors for traffic updates and reroutes you to avoid jams. Imagine if Waze earned commissions to keep you on the road longer. It would not be nearly as efficient.

That being said, Waze isn't perfect, and hiring a fiduciary advisor won't solve all of your problems. It's just that you will get fleeced the least. The fiduciary standard disallows factors that don't help portfolio performance but line the pockets of brokers and firms. So before you hire an advisor, look into their registrations, compensation model, credentials, and legal history to ensure you'll be getting not only advice but also advocacy.

UNDERSTAND YOUR OBJECTIVES

When a client walks through my door with money ready to invest, they are usually eager to talk strategy. Before we get to investment vehicles and asset allocation, we have to talk through goals and objectives. Does this client want to save? Does he want tax-free income? Does he want to retire early? Identifying goals helps clients focus, prepare for the journey, and stay the course.

If a client comes in and says, "Safety is all that's important to me," I'll dig deeper into his situation to test the veracity of that statement. Let's imagine he has $2 million saved up and only two years before retirement, but he is adamant that he'll need $150,000 per year to spend until he dies. He doesn't have any other sources of income, nor is he willing to postpone his retirement. That means he's looking for a 7.5 percent distribution rate; he'd have to be 100 percent invested in stocks to have a chance at hitting that goal. Well, then, if safety is his only objective, something else will have to give; he may have to retire later or cut expenses in half. If he can't reconcile all of this, he won't be successful.

Factors such as savings, income, retirement age, risk tolerance, cash requirements for building a house, paying for kids' college, history of health problems, and so on must get their stage time in the conversation. Once they're addressed, someone has to come in and draw lines to make sure everything matches based on the time horizon. At the end of the day, clients benefit from someone else stepping in to help them understand when their goals don't align with their expectations and requirements.

UNDERSTAND YOUR RISK APPETITE

One of the most profound things an advisor can do for you is to help you assess your risk-tolerance level.

Let's say a client walks in with $3 million and a stated willingness to endure a 15 percent loss since they're "a long-term investor." I want to know how they really tolerate that level of loss. How would they feel about a year-end statement coming in the mail that informs them that their $3 million is now worth about $2.5 million, then another one coming in the next year saying their fortune is now worth less than $2.2 million? That's the equivalent of a 15 percent loss, two years in a row, and in the end, $3 million becoming about $2 million. How does *that* feel to them? Because 15 percent, 30 percent, whatever, looks a whole lot different in actual money than it does in a hypothetical. This conversation often puts a horrified look on a client's face. Turns out, they don't really have the risk appetite they thought they did. As Mike Tyson said, "Everybody has a plan until they get hit in the mouth."

Another thing to consider is the fact that different seasons of life will change risk appetites, and you need to keep tabs on where you fall and learn how to adjust. Let's say the same $3-million client walks through my door at age 70, very confident in their risk appetite, and hops into the market with their money on July 1. Then an unpredictable market downturn begins on August 1. It would be natural for the client to jump into worst-case scenario thinking, "I'm going to outlive my money!" So this 70-year-old certainly doesn't have a 30 percent downside risk appetite. Their stated risk appetite was born of wishful thinking because they would love the juicier returns that can only come from a riskier position. Yet they cannot actually stomach a 30 percent loss. There is a reasonable tradeoff between risk and reward, and it's possible to construct a portfolio that reflects a client's true appetite. When people try to make tactical allocations that either overrepresent or underrepresent their risk profile, they're likely to find out the hard way that their eyes are bigger than their stomachs.

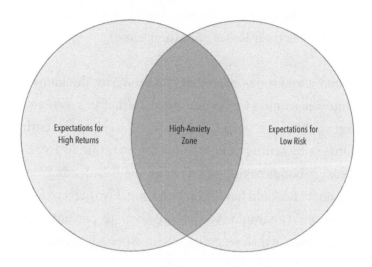

Anyone who thinks they can anticipate the "next turn" in the market or the direction of interest rates, etc., is likely overestimating their capabilities. The variables are so numerous that no one can predict what's next. But since the stock market rises 81 percent of the time, a bet on the market should never be lifted. It should also be tackled with a percentage of one's net worth that can withstand whatever variables the market throws at it. In 2000, and again in 2008, stocks lost half their value in short order. Most people who brag about having properly moved their chess pieces prior are either forgetful or deceiving themselves. The moves are so choppy and abrupt in both directions; navigating perfectly is nearly impossible. Professional and amateur investors alike failed to reinvest at the bottom, whereas long-term investors remained invested the entire time and, as the market corrected, gained back their losses (and then some).

What if I told you in 2007 that I had some inside skinny on what was coming to the mortgage market in 2008–2009 and could plot a perfect path for you to skirt the entire damage by selling your stocks and investing in 10-year Treasury bonds paying 5 percent annually instead? Would you do it? It would have been tempting. Five percent for 10 years would guarantee you a more-than-50-percent cumulative return, which seems excellent, especially considering what happened in the stock market.

But even including losing 53 percent in the 16 months during the '08–'09 housing crisis, the math says no, the Treasury bonds, even predicted at the right time, sidestepping all the carnage, would *still* not be a better choice over the stock market. If you had owned the S&P 500 (starting in early 2008 and exiting in 2018), by the start of 2016, you would have recouped all your losses from 2008 and gained 50 percent more, already achieving the bonds' promised returns for the full 10 years. Plus, those last two years (2016 and 2017) would have propelled you 30 percent past the return on the Treasury bonds. By 2018, you would have earned a 102 percent return on stocks compared to 50 percent on bonds, and that's before you consider that the interest earned on the bonds was taxable at up to 39.8

percent and the stock dividends were half as taxable or less. The stocks actually finished that nasty 10-year period as nearly a 3-to-1 winner when you also consider taxes.

Despite bonds' miserable returns with current interest rates so low, they actually have a useful purpose for investors. Their job is to simply "not be a stock." Bonds are tradeable loans with finite risks, and for some individual investors, a bond matches well with their risk appetite.

All individual investors would be wise to find a spot on the risk curve that is comfortable for them if (and when) things get bad. A curveball *will* come your way. You can't always anticipate it. You won't always take the perfect swing to hit the ball right on the money. Wise investors understand that they cannot see the next curveball, and neither can their advisor. When a 50 percent slide in stocks comes, how much can you handle before you cry uncle? Most people find comfort in having half to three-quarters of their money at risk and the rest in something safe, like a bond. (Again, this has a great deal to do with many other factors such as: Is your home paid for? Is your job secure? Will you inherit money later in life? Do you own company stock in concentration? Do you have life insurance? Is your spouse employable in your absence?)

It's the job of people like me to test the waters and help find a balance between your goals and your risk tolerance.

For someone whose risk tolerance is low, I can build a portfolio that is very unlikely to ever lose any value, but it will also never produce a competitive rate of return. There's a tradeoff. So we must deal with the gap between perception and reality and the underlying question of risk appetite under duress.

The crux of the matter is whether one will cut and run at the next market swoon. Many individual investors won't fess up to what a nervous ninny they are until they've already lost a significant portion of their investment. This is because they're not sure what kind of investor they are to begin with. A truly risk-averse investor might step into riskier territory only to run for cover when the action gets too hot. They would actually be better off just sticking their money (or a portion of it) in a fixed account or bonds and avoiding the heartache that will surely come from risky assets. When that heartache comes, the risk-averse investor, in over their head, will bail out of their risky stock investments, thus denying their stocks a recovery, which makes an overall loss inevitable. Don't misunderstand me here. The problem is not the fact that stocks have downsides; it's the investor's inability to digest the downsides, which leads them to take corrective action at the wrong times in order to make themselves feel better. Allowing this pattern to go on unchecked is the road to perdition. Don't go there. The best advisors earn their living by talking investors out of things, not into things.

Accountability, at the moment of a serious downtick or crash, is where an advisor can be worth their weight in gold. These might be the most valuable words ever spoken to you: "Ms. Jones, getting aggressive after the big stock run-up seems to be an awful idea because you liquidated your stocks in 2008, didn't you?"

TWO-PORTFOLIO THEORY

A simple step can aid but not cure an unwillingness to accept downside risks: compartmentalization. Having separate buckets for your higher-risk and lower-risk assets can be particularly powerful in reducing the fear of missing out (FOMO) by appeasing the need to balance safety with the desire for higher returns. This process is what I call the two-portfolio theory. Imagine the relief one might feel if, when their risky pool loses half its value, they also have an entirely separate account immune to that same risk. Even the exercise of separating the two into different accounts can provide relief. When "risk" and "no risk" assets are mixed in a single account, there tends to be emotional contamination. We often lose our sense of perspective as to what is causing our distress. We can't determine the flavor we don't like in our spaghetti when we don't know whether it's the sauce or the noodle that tastes sour. Perspective is easier to maintain when we can see the buckets clearly. I suggest a sauce bowl and a noodle bowl.

A higher-risk account might be full of stocks (or stock mutual funds or ETFs). Coupling a higher-risk account with a lower-risk one (containing muni bonds, cash, CDs, or other highly predictable securities) can work wonders to provide peace of mind for the timid. It's even a good idea for the not so timid because it can help with evaluating performance. You can get a much more rational and granular look at returns when they are distilled down to their finest form. Keeping high-risk and low-risk assets in separate accounts requires that distillation. A mixture of stocks and a separate mixture of bonds come to mind because these two different markets rarely have much in common, and they are the building blocks of investment portfolios of all shapes and sizes. It's the characteristic differentiation of risks that allows these often-opposing forces to peacefully coexist in most investors' overall action plan. These buckets should be proportioned according to one's personal goals and expectations. Don't forget, your expectations need to be reasonable. Outsized expectations are often a precursor to trouble.

CHAPTER EIGHT

PORTFOLIO CONSTRUCTION

"Don't just do something, stand there!"

—MAX HERZSTEIN, OUR MOST QUOTABLE CLIENT

If you've made it this far, you've done the hard work and are now ready to move on to the fun part: makin' money.

As we pivot to discussing important points in portfolio construction, I want to focus on the central themes and not some formula or exploitable niche. It's pretty clear that if there is an exploitable niche for us, it's the unceasing errors others make when serving ego, fear, and greed. That's why you will hear many advisors describe their methodology as a black box (where magical returns simply appear), but the description that entices people the most is the idea of a one-way plumbing valve.

If you own a sprinkler system connected to a well or a city water line, building code requires you to have "back-flow prevention device." Backflow from your yard could contaminate the city water supply with waste, so this mechanism is often a flapper valve that allows water to flow only in one direction. In the investment realm, many brokers promise something similar: an account where the money only flows in. But only a fixed account with nominal returns can do that. Any product that looks like a one-way plumbing valve (and many are often just an illusion or an aberration) will rely on you not fully under-standing its drawbacks.

In 1996, Long Term Capital had a pitch in which they claimed to have created the holy grail of investing. They applied leverage to a reliable and long-standing quirk in the marketplace, exploiting a seemingly riskless opportu-nity. They used borrowed money to buy bonds, which they promised to sell back in the short term (also known as a repurchase agreement, or "repo"). They rode this animal to spectacular returns for the two years prior to 1998, when the quirk suddenly vanished. But it wasn't the end of the quirk that created the problems; it was the lever-age. Applying the theory with borrowed money left Long Term Capital investors with tens of billions in losses and their hair on fire. The whole thing blew up in their faces, wiping out all prior gains and the principal to boot. This happened again in 2019 with the UBS Yield Enhancement

Strategy, cutely dubbed "YES." This was an option strategy that clients could tack on to their existing accounts and obtain a "yield," with their accounts held as collateral. They didn't even have to put any money in. "Let's just use your account as collateral against this 'easy' money strategy. It's easy money just sitting there waiting to be picked up by someone. Might as well be you, Mr. Jones." Poof! More hair on fire. Two years later, this quirk vaporized overnight, and UBS clients lost $1 billion.

It's not the promise of no downside that is the problem here. Treasury bills, money funds, and short-duration munis all offer virtually zero risk and virtually zero return. They're honest about that. The problem areas are the other constructs that promise no downside and disproportionate returns. It's that "something for nothing" concoction that is so appealing and so dangerous.

I understand the investor's dilemma and mindset. It's totally natural to approach the investment world with little information and think, *All I really need to do is find some super-smart fellow who can create some vehicle that doesn't ever decline. Two-percent returns on munis are boring. All I want is stock returns with bond safety features. That's not too much to ask.*

This investor is a sitting duck for self-inflicted misery and hucksters making promises of easy money and low risks.

Rather than rely on adding value through fancy decision making, let's acknowledge the difficulty of outsmarting the totality of all other investors. Remember that whatever you are buying, there has to be a seller on the other side of the deal. Are they really that much less intelligent than you? You might be able to outsmart someone uneducated. You might also get lucky and make a smart stock pick occasionally. But being able to outsmart all the other professionals in the room routinely? I'm smart enough to know I'm not that smart, and neither are you, nor is your broker. Investors are better off "picking and sticking." Pick a broad strategy, and don't deviate. There are two ways to pick-and-stick. One is on a risk level, and one is on a strategy level, which we will explore in a bit.

As we discussed in the last chapter, very few individual investors are good at being objective about themselves, which is why a good advisor can make a significant difference when it comes to honest risk-tolerance assessment. Getting this personal risk-tolerance assessment wrong can lead to a host of performance-robbing consequences, including:

- Investor anxiety
- Advisor switching
- Portfolio trading/turnover
- Taxes and extra fees
- Indecisiveness

- Goal switching
- Performance chasing
- Losing sight of tomorrow because we're still trying to fix yesterday

Proper risk assessment can't be overstated; getting it right is the single most important part of investing.

BUILDING BLOCKS

Before we dive into how to construct your portfolio, it's important to understand the basic building blocks. You're going to need to have some conversations with yourself and with your advisor regarding different investment vehicles and what to expect from them. Below are the main building blocks that make up a typical investor's portfolio. Let's get down to it.

STOCKS

Ownership of stocks (ownership in a company and entitlement to its profits) and bonds (loans to a company or municipality and entitlement to fixed payments and a return of principal after a finite period) come with their own sets of risks. For stocks, the risks that belong to the company (e.g., their product becoming obsolete, a founder dying, a new competitor taking market share, etc.) can be catastrophic, potentially leading to the downfall of the company and the complete loss of invested capital. Larger, older companies tend to prepare for and withstand these risks better than new companies. Yet, even they are often disrupted by things leadership did not anticipate. Kodak once thought that digital photography was a passing fad. Instead, the sudden lack of need for film nearly obliterated the company. Blockbuster made the same mistake when they passed on the opportunity to buy Netflix for $50 million. Now the streaming service has a market capitalization of around $200 billion. The upside to owning individual companies belongs to the stockholders. Often, a portion of earnings goes to stockholders in the form of dividends (which are taxed at half the rate of other income) and the success of the company leads to increased stock prices, thus raising the value of the investment.

Stocks represent a shared interest in the business. That's why they're sold in "shares." And when it comes to wealth accumulation, stock ownership in companies is where the action is. Entrepreneurs who start companies are able to accumulate a lot of wealth because in a sense, starting a company is making a concentrated "investment" and owning your own "stock." Make no mistake, it's a risky position. Many entrepreneurs have a few big failures before they succeed. There's truth in the old saying, "Nothing ventured, nothing gained." Making large bets in a few companies is one of the only ways to gain market-beating returns. This concentration also exposes you to the highest level of risk you can experience as a stock investor. Billionaire Mark Cuban has stated that he has close to a billion dollars in Amazon stock, and given his estimated $4.1 billion net worth, that's nearly a quarter of his wealth tied up in one company. I consider that a pretty sizable bet. He's a gutsy investor who got rich making bets like this.

However, many people get the mistaken impression that investing in stocks is inherently dangerous. Surely, investments in individual companies are riskier than those in a mixture of companies, and we are all keenly aware of spectacular flameouts like Enron. Yes, even diversified stock portfolios are subject to periodic swings, but the *averages* are relatively stable over time. Some of this riskiness is merely about perception since stocks are not much riskier than other forms of ownership such as real estate, which is perceived to be more stable. The mere fact that we can instantly know what our stocks are worth makes them *seem* riskier than other forms of ownership. But just because we know the price doesn't make it more volatile than that which we cannot see. By-the-minute quotes aren't available for other, seemingly stable assets like your home, but I would bet that value fluctuates quite a bit.

Another reason that investors often perceive stocks to be dangerous is that they might be mistaking a speculation for an investment. Many would-be investors never recover from the psychological damage of watching their "life savings" vanish before their eyes when they bet on some untested "unicorn" business. Imagine the impression that could leave on a 22-year-old investing their first $600 paycheck on some fly-by-night drug company supposedly coming up with the next big thing. A tax deduction is a small consolation prize for that trauma, and maybe they decide stocks aren't for them. But that is a bit like deciding you don't like food because your first taste was liver.

Investors tend to deal with individual holdings with suspicion because the risk level is higher than that of a similar fund. One thing to remember is the concept of beta, which I mentioned in Chapter 3. Beta is market exposure. One way to quantify the riskiness of a particular stock is to determine its beta. We can assume the S&P 500 has a beta of 1 since it is often used to represent the market. So a stock with a beta of 1 moves in lockstep with the S&P. A stock with a beta of 1.2 would rise and fall 20 percent more than the S&P.

A mutual fund or an ETF (which we'll talk about below) brings investor ownership together in a pool. Stock funds normally hold shares from many companies, and therefore the attributes of each individual company get blended among those of the other holdings in proportion. Each company added causes more and more dilution of the attributes of the others. With enough holdings, the beta will eventually become 1. This blending has a calming effect on investors because clearly the riskiness of the pool is lower than the riskiness of each component. There is also not as much emotional agitation when you see that one of your stocks is down 30 percent. That loss in one stock may not have any real bearing on an overall portfolio depending on how the rest is allocated, but it's often a thorn in the side of the investor who doesn't know how to contextualize it. The lack of single-stock agitation can keep investors in their seats longer, which naturally defers taxes and adds to compounded return. This also tends to minimize mistakes because the fewer times you act or react, the fewer opportunities you have to mess up. Wealth managers often prefer to use funds for those reasons when constructing client portfolios. Some firms like ours also build client portfolios with individual stocks because that can have other offsetting benefits, mostly with tax strategy, especially when the client has already demonstrated their ability to be innately calm through a big-picture lens.

BONDS

Bonds are helpful when used as ice cubes to cool down a scalding cup of coffee. They have predictable outcomes, whereas stocks generally do not. Bonds are essentially loans that you can trade. The terms of a bond (coupon rate, maturity, etc.) are set from the beginning and go largely unchanged as the bond matures. Prices can change during the bond's term because of environmental shifts.

If a bond's coupon rate (the guaranteed rate of payment received back from the bond issuer), which is already set until maturity, is deemed uncompetitive, the price falls. That's why long-term bonds, let's say 30-year bonds, experience lots of price volatility over time. When a bond with a 3 percent coupon rate is up for sale in a 4 percent pricing environment, the price that a buyer would be willing to pay is lower, fully discounting the present value of all the years that the new buyer won't get that extra percentage point. The same thing happens in reverse when rates fall.

But nothing is guaranteed. What if a company that issued bonds is involved in a major lawsuit? That could hurt bond prices because the chance you won't get your money back is higher. But in the end, bonds are still safer: stock shareholders get wiped out first, and the bondholders receive what's left of the company's equity in liquidation, as would any other creditor.

Municipal bonds are issued to support the infrastructure of local communities. School districts, bridges, toll road authorities, and so forth are all allowed to issue municipal bonds. Interest earned by investors in these bonds is normally tax-free because the federal government understands the benefits of local administration and local responsibility for local interests. Municipal bonds normally pay proportionally lower interest rates accordingly. Yet, that was not the case in 2018 and 2019, when munis often yielded more than taxable equivalents despite their additional tax benefit. I use the term *equivalent* loosely because munis truly have no equal. Despite the fragmented nature of more than 200,000 different issues in the marketplace, munis are highly sought after by investors. Tax avoidance is one attraction. Another is the remarkable resilience of muni bond issues. They are far less likely to go belly up than corporate bonds of similar quality because payments come from the tax base, and since property owners are required and incentivized to pay their taxes, the neighborhood is quite unlikely to fail. As a matter of fact, a muni bond is 40 times less likely to default than a similarly rated corporate bond.

Munis are harder to trade, but for buy-and-hold investors, their quirky market is more than tolerable given their safety and tax-free nature, along with competitive returns.

MUTUAL FUNDS

Many investors choose to hold individual stocks or bonds such as Microsoft or Coca-Cola, and there are many good reasons for that. Even more investors choose to hold those securities inside of a mutual fund. Investors generally believe that funds are the easiest and simplest way to invest, and that's generally true. A mutual fund is simply an aggregation tool that lets you commingle assets with other investors. Each investor buys into a central pool and can leave with their loot whenever they want. This structure allows investors to attain risk-reducing diversification without researching and purchasing tens or hundreds of individual securities. A trustee of the fund administers all the legalities, including auditing and accounting for the comings and goings of cash. Normally, a professional manager is charged with sticking to a particular strategy for the fund, which is outlined in the offering documents or prospectus. For these services, they charge fees.

Two of the largest mutual fund providers, Fidelity and Vanguard, illustrate the variety of mutual fund offerings. Vanguard is known for its low-cost and mostly indexed funds, whereas Fidelity is one of the highest-cost fund families. That's because Fidelity has built a reputation for high-performing funds (by heavily marketing their winning funds) and offers what are called open-end mutual funds. When you hear someone talking about a mutual fund, they're most likely referring to an open-end fund. These funds have true shared accounting, meaning the comings and goings of other investors impact the taxation of all investors in the fund. Open-end funds are most often actively managed, meaning the holdings of securities within the fund change frequently. Sounds expensive. This activity also creates tax drag. Again, expensive. Vanguard, on the other hand, offers closed-end ETFs in addition to open-end funds. For decades, mutual funds were the go-to vehicle for the majority of investors. That was true until

2019 when the assets of these closed-end ETFs actually eclipsed their open-end brethren.

VANGUARD VS. FIDELITY

You might not know this, but Vanguard is actually a nonprofit. They technically operate as a true "mutual company," which means it is formed as a "shared-at-cost" structure with shareholders. The actual corporate ownership of Vanguard belongs to the people who invest in their funds, whereas Fidelity is owned by the billionaire Johnson family. Since Vanguard is technically larger than Fidelity, those same "billions" of implied equity value from Vanguard ownership truly resides inside the accounts of their fund shareholders who have saved that fee money for themselves.

ETFS

There are advantages to combining your money with that of other investors as long as you can avoid the natural tax disadvantages of their choices. That is exactly what an exchange-traded fund (ETF) can allow you to do that a traditional open-end mutual fund cannot. An ETF is essentially a mutual fund that trades like a stock and is listed on an exchange, where its value is driven by the value of its holdings. ETFs are famously low cost because most are managed passively, tracking an index.

It's no wonder that ETF sales have been booming. But

my favorite thing about ETFs is their tax treatment due to two structural attributes: (1) Most ETFs subscribe to index methodology, which only rarely requires repositioning; this cuts down on taxable activity. (2) ETFs shed untraceable gains into the marketplace rather than onto a shareholder's taxable Form 1099 like a traditional mutual fund would. That is because unlike open-end mutual funds, ETFs don't allow investors to enter or exit the fund with cash. Buying the ETF requires bringing the component stocks with you. Selling happens the same way, in reverse. This "share creation" happens behind the scenes and is invisible to the investor, but it has a vital manifestation: it avoids taxable distributions. If you sell your ETF shares, your cost basis remains what you paid for it (or very close to what you paid for it) years ago, or maybe even decades ago, and your activity impacts you alone. But remember that if you sell your mutual fund shares, your activity affects all of the fund's investors. Every year, your mutual fund's 1099 reflects your proportionate holdings and your share of the tax burden (caused by the comings and goings of other investors in the fund and by the position changes during the year), which erodes long-term compounding of your return. That is why a 20-year-old mutual fund holding may be worth five times what you paid for it, but most of the gain has likely already been taxed many years ago. A comparable ETF would have kept pace in performance (or even surpassed due to lower costs) and maintained the unrealized gain.

As an example, we have a mutual fund on our books that was originally purchased in 2006 for $20,000. The value has since grown to $82,154. Simple math would lead you to believe there is a $62,154 gain. Yet, the statement shows that the original $20,000 purchase now has a cost basis of $76,334. How is it that the "cost" grew by $56,334? That is the effect of the taxable gains distributed (and taxed) in prior years. We have a similar ETF position on our books, which also had a $20,000 purchase price at about the same time in 2006. That holding is worth roughly $90,000 in mid-2020 today (the difference owed mostly to better performance from lower fees). But what stands in stark contrast to the mutual fund is that the "cost" now shows as $20,660, with a $69,340 untaxed gain (which might be taxed later if we sell our position). The prior distributions from the open-end mutual fund cost the investor $13,400 in taxes ($56,334 multiplied by the 23.8 percent capital gains tax rate), plus the loss of compounding on the $13,400. This unnecessary "prepayment" of taxes in the mutual fund also neuters the powerful Step-Up in Basis Rule at the time of an investor's death. The structure of the ETF allows the step-up to be used to full effect, in this case, cleansing the holding from almost $70,000 in gain. Thus, the ETF is the better compounder on all fronts: lower internal fees, less tax drag from premature taxes paid, and retention of a possible tax-free step-up on the entire gain.

Before we head into deeper waters, we have to talk about what could be a substantial hole in the bottom of your boat: taxes. Yes, you may be accustomed to paying taxes on the returns you garner, but there are ways to gain superior tax treatment. Tax deferral is often presented as an undisputed benefit rightly pursued because "surely, putting off taxes is always a good idea..." Although seeking tax deferral is generally good advice, it certainly shouldn't drive all your investment decisions. A key to understanding tax-deferral strategy is to recognize that any tax-deferred income, such as in an IRA, 401(k), annuity, and so forth will be taxed as ordinary income when it comes out. I say, pay Caesar what is due him but no more and no sooner than required.

So how do you build a tax strategy? At a basic level, you should weigh the tax rate that will apply in your accumulation years against that which will apply in your retirement. In fact, the only way tax deferral can be a great benefit to you is if you are in a high tax bracket during accumulation and a low tax bracket during retirement. Any other combination has much less benefit, if any. Plus, this combination is rare anyway since very high earners tend to be those whose investment earnings (and ordinary income tax rate) remain high in retirement.

It is possible to optimally allocate your assets among your

tax-deferred and taxable account types. Yet, because tax advice is unique in each situation, I'll give you just one example of a case in which practical advice flouts conventional wisdom in hopes this will make you assess your own situation a little more vigorously.

Convention dictates that high-growth vehicles should be placed in a tax-deferred account such as an IRA, which is protected from taxes for most of your lifetime. That means you can reinvest any gains you earn so they compound over time without the drag of taxes. This works well until it's time to pay the IRS, when all gains distributed from an IRA are taxed at your ordinary income tax rate, which can be as high as 39.8 percent!

So what if, instead, you put your low-growth assets in your IRA and your high-growth assets in a regular taxable account? In that case, your high-growth assets might be exposed to occasional capital gains taxation at a maximum tax rate of 23.8 percent (but that shouldn't be a huge concern with a passively managed strategy in place). Remember that when you die, the Step-Up in Basis Rule passes all of the assets in your taxable account (not your IRA) to your inheritors tax-free. I'm sure you can imagine the profound advantage of having your highest growth assets (using a low-turnover methodology) shooting for a step-up at death. You wouldn't want that advantage to be lost on low-growth assets like bonds.

The illustration below shows the conventional allocation method (high-growth assets in the IRA) compared to the tax-optimized allocation method (high-growth assets in a taxable account). With $100,000 in each account at the

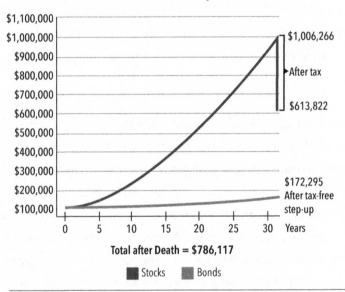

Conventional Allocation Method

$100,000 IRA invested in high-growth assets (i.e., stocks),
$100,000 taxable account invested in low-growth assets (i.e., bonds)

$1,006,266

After tax

$613,822

$172,295
After tax-free
step-up

Total after Death = $786,117

■ Stocks   ■ Bonds

Assumptions:

Beginning IRA value = $100,000
Beginning taxable account value = $100,000
Stock/bond mix @ 50/50
Death = 30 years

Stocks @ 8% return,
including 2% dividends
Bonds @ 3% return

start, the difference in outcomes is massive. Assuming death in 30 years, the heirs of the tax-optimized allocation will inherit 30 percent (nearly $250,000) more.

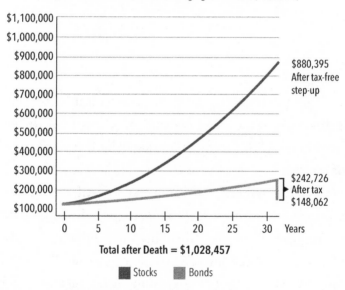

Tax-Optimized Allocation Method

$100,000 IRA invested in low-growth assets (i.e., bonds),
$100,000 taxable account invested in high-growth assets (i.e., stocks)

$880,395
After tax-free step-up

$242,726
After tax
$148,062

Total after Death = $1,028,457

■ Stocks   ■ Bonds

Tax rate on dividends = 23.8%
Tax rate on capital gains = 23.8%
Tax rate on ordinary income = 39.8%
Tax rate on gains in taxable account at death = 0%
Tax rate on gains in tax-deferred account at death = 37.9%

Precious Metals

Many money managers will pitch their clients on various vehicles that have less appealing tax treatment. One example of a product with poor treatment is precious metals, like gold. Metals offer a good hedge against your other investments since they tend to have lower beta, performing better when the stock market is in decline. However, precious metals are considered collectibles and thus gains are taxed at 28 percent when sold. Metals also generate a negative dividend because these investments have physical storage costs.

Commodities

Another pitch you might hear is for commodities like natural gas, oil, or beef because they, too, tend to lack correlation with the stock market. There are a number of reasons why most investors should just say no. Many commodity holdings are required to utilize mark-to-market accounting, which requires periodic settlement of taxes even if the investment has not been sold. Just the increase in value could be taxable every year. Commodities are also a "non-price-trending" asset, meaning they don't consistently rise in price like stocks. They bob and weave and gyrate, meaning that holding them requires a "trading-centric" methodology. We have already discussed the drawbacks of trading-centric methods. The chance of making big mistakes is high, the taxes are high, the fees are high, and there would likely never be a step-up in basis to make any of it tax-free. Not to mention, these can be highly illiquid and crazy pricing results are possible, as when oil futures in April 2020 traded at negative value; for a few weeks, you had to pay someone to take your oil off your hands.

Annuities

Annuities are another product category that seems to offer tax advantages. The pitch normally touts guaranteed perpetual income and tax-deferred accumulation. Yes, but annuities pay returns as ordinary income and don't qualify for the more beneficial capital gains tax treatment. Ever. This can allow taxes to consume nearly 40 percent of the return. If you're choosing deferral, you must agree to ordinary income taxation eventually, forfeiting any other tax benefit such as the Step-Up in Basis Rule at death. The IRS isn't stupid, and they know they will outlive you. Make your choices wisely.

The forfeiture of other significant tax benefits in choosing the tax deferral of an annuity is not often outlined to investors. Let's talk about what you might be missing. Stocks held outside of an annuity can be sold in small pieces with taxable gains attached to each piece proportionately. Conversely, all annuities distribute gains first. For example, let's say a $100,000 purchase of an annuity and a $100,000 purchase of an ETF eventually have the same 50 percent increase in value, making them each worth $150,000. Selling $15,000 of the ETF would show a $5,000 capital gain and $10,000 of original principal because the taxable portion is distributed evenly. The maximum tax on the capital gain is currently 23.8 percent, which comes to $1,190 on the $5,000 portion. In contrast, taking $15,000 from the annuity would be fully taxable on the entire amount since gains come out first. The whole $15,000 is taxed at your ordinary income tax rate, which can be as high as 39.8 percent. That's a $5,670 tax bill on a $15,000 withdrawal from an annuity compared to $1,190 in an ETF. (Stocks have the same tax treatment as ETFs.) So much for "valuable" tax deferral! Furthermore, annuities are notorious for having high costs and juicy commissions for their salesmen. There's an old industry joke that says, "Annuities are not bought; they are sold." The implication is that most people need to be convinced that an annuity is a wise purchase. I believe far more people own annuities than otherwise would if they fully understood the drawbacks.

THE ANNUITY EXCEPTION

There are circumstances for which an annuity is the right tool for the job. I've recommended annuities to lower-income-earning older people for whom the threat of outliving their assets is very real and who also don't have time to allow a downturn in the market to recover. An annuity's poor tax treatment isn't such a big deal for someone in the lower tax brackets who is likely less concerned with how large a nest egg they will leave to their inheritors. These folks need the higher growth attributes of stocks, but one big market swoon could permanently unseat them. A variable-rate annuity will allow them to add a "guaranteed lifetime withdrawal benefit" to their account for a fee, essentially allowing them to buy insurance against the detrimental effects of a market swoon. Their income is guaranteed for life and can only increase. Fortunately, this kind of annuity is available in low-cost versions, but you're not likely to hear about it since there's no money in it for salespeople.

LET'S TALK STRATEGY

The process of piecing together a portfolio made up of assets of varying risk levels is a very personal one, so it wouldn't be fair to try to address every reader's unique situation with one broad stroke. Instead, I'll give the most valuable advice I can on your strategy going forward.

MODERN PORTFOLIO THEORY

The distinction between asset allocation (choosing the ratio of each asset class, or more finely, market sector, you will hold in your portfolio) and security selection is lost on most. But the work of a few prominent economists indicates that by merely looking at the math of risk and probability, it quickly becomes apparent that in fact, security selection is probably the least important factor in returns. Instead, we have to look at asset allocation. Harry Markowitz theorized about this idea in his writings "Portfolio Selection" (1952) and "Portfolio Selection: Efficient Diversification" (1959), for which he shared the Nobel Prize in Economics with William Sharpe in 1990. Sharpe's contribution came from his 1964 writings on what came to be known as the capital asset pricing model (CAPM). Markowitz's and Sharpe's works have been blended together into what is today called modern portfolio theory (MPT).

In summary, MPT holds that it is possible to construct an optimal portfolio, maximizing returns, given a certain level of risk. Its authors discovered that certain blends of unrelated asset classes create portfolios with optimal risk-reward characteristics, irrespective of security selection within any asset class. This often manifests in an investor's asset allocation in a stock, bond, and cash blend but could also include more specific "silos" such as small-capitalization stocks. Optimization often favors rotating into the most distressed or cheapest group per the CAPM part of the model. This theory meshes well with using Callan's Periodic Table (discussed below) to shop for next year's likely winner off the bottom of the menu.

With the introduction of the first index fund in 1974 and its modern iteration, the ETF, in 1993, Markowitz and Sharpe are surely gleeful. These low-cost and tax-efficient portfolios are a perfect fit as building blocks in an allocation-minded approach to efficient portfolio construction. So while brokers build showy and expensive ladders in an attempt to harvest fruit from the tops of the tallest trees in the orchard and clients watch, clamor, and cheer, the sweetest fruit is dropping to the ground below, where you can safely pick it up with nary a squabble.

CONSIDER ACTIVE VS. PASSIVE MANAGEMENT

The trend toward passive investment management is steadily accelerating. This style of management typically uses mutual funds and ETFs to mirror the holdings of a market index and, more simply, refers to buying a large cross-section of the marketplace and making few or no changes to holdings over time. Active management involves constantly tweaking of the stock positions held and buying individual stocks based on a philosophy or a set of factors. These factors make up the "special sauce" of the portfolio manager. But do they actually deliver incremental performance? The results usually don't justify the fees. The lights have gotten brighter on this reality and the additional scrutiny on actively managed products has put negative pressure on the fees active managers are charging. And so, investors are migrating in large numbers to passive-management choices with lower embedded costs.

Everyone wants "superior" performance. So let's discuss it. Superior performance is easier to accomplish by deciding to be average but paying less to acquire those average returns, making one above-average after costs are considered. But when most people hear "average," they think of being in the middle of the pack. Yet, above average in this case simply means migrating to the top of the pack by way of sitting tight while everyone else makes mistakes and actively trades, increasing their fees and costs along the way. That's why indexed investments, which are normally passively managed, usually outperform 90 percent[32] of their actively managed peers. There's an old legend that says that the only one who made money in the California 1849 gold rush was Levi Strauss. So it is with passive investing. Most individual investors (professionals, too) are focused on the gold they can find through a smart trade, but I see the gold they spill (through costs, fees, taxes, and mistakes) while they're looking for their eureka moment. Since the markets are a closed ecosystem, meaning all the money stays within it, the money that gets lost in all the frenetic trading naturally goes to those who sit tight with passive-management investment strategies.

BE ABOVE AVERAGE

Another reason the "average" is so far "above average" is a statistical aberration called positive skew. When you have lots of very average components in a group and just a few

32 Berlinda Liu, "SPIVA® U.S. Year-End 2019," SPIVA® U.S. Year-End 2019—S&P Dow Jones Indices, 2019, https://www.spglobal.com/spdji/en/spiva/article/spiva-us-year-end-2019/.

are head and shoulders above the rest, the average skews higher than the median. The average net worth of residents of Omaha, Nebraska, is skewed because the town's most famous resident, Warren Buffett, has a net worth of $81 billion. That makes the average appear quite a bit higher than it would be otherwise. There are only 468,262 residents of Omaha, meaning that Warren's net worth alone adds $173,000 to each resident's average net worth.

Let's do a little mental math experiment. Visualize a purple Crown Royal bag with nine poker chips inside. The chips are all white, and each one represents a value of eight. If you were to pick all nine, you would have a total value of 72. Now let's say we add a tenth chip, a red one, with a value of 100. The value of the whole bag is now 172, making the technical average value of a chip 17.2. However, blindly selecting one at random from the bag would make your odds of outperformance (choosing the red chip) only one in ten. Nine out of ten times, if you selected only one chip, you would actually *underperform* the average by grabbing one of the lower value chips. This is roughly how the math works out for the average stock mutual fund. If you wanted to make sure you did well, which would require you to grab the red chip, the best option would be to select the entire bag. Otherwise, you're taking a 90 percent chance that you will underperform average, and only a 10 percent chance that you will snag that red chip and beat the market. (And of course, that's before you consider fees and taxes, which make the math far worse.)

Now let's make the example even more like the real world and apply it to chips and stocks. Suppose you now have a pillowcase full of chips. We also have a new color chip: blue, which has a value of only one. Let's add 100 of those blue ones to the bag. Let's also add a dozen more of those valuable red chips worth 100 each. Then let's add 3,500 more white chips, much like the total number of listed stocks in the United States. If you are playing the game by choosing your chips one at a time, you will get swamped by the person betting on the entire bag because they are *guaranteeing* they will own all 13 of the high-performing red chips.

MAINTAINING MARKET HARMONY

Total US assets in passive strategies finally surpassed those in active strategies in August 2019, and today the two strategies have roughly the same value of assets. Some people are concerned about the mass adoption of passive management because active managers keep the market in better harmony.[33] However, because active strategies still control a significant portion of US assets, I think any danger posed from the disappearance of active managers still seems a long way off. It also seems unlikely since the minute the balance swings too heavily toward passive management, active managers will swoop in and capture any pricing disparity, serving to keep market efficiency alive and well.

---

33   Tom Lauricella and Gabrielle DiBenedetto, "A Look at the Road to Asset Parity between Passive and Active U.S. Funds," Morningstar, Inc., June 12, 2019, https://www.morningstar.com/insights/2019/06/12/asset-parity.

For an illustration, we can look to Warren Buffett and a bet he made in 2007. Warren Buffett is one of the world's top-five richest men, depending on the day you look. He made his money managing Berkshire Hathaway, a large insurance conglomerate. He remains convinced that choosing securities is fraught with peril when compared to buying the averages for all stocks. He was so convinced of the laws of randomness and of the performance drag that was created by the costs of smart people making too many (often poor) investment choices that he challenged the hedge fund industry to a friendly wager. (Hedge fund managers are notoriously the best stock pickers.) Warren's bet was that a grouping of smart hedge funds would get outrun by a static investment in the stock market index over the course of a decade. His challenge was taken up by Protégé Partners who chose five hedge funds to make up their portfolio. Warren and Protégé wagered $1 million each and the winner of the bet would get to choose which charity received the $2 million pot. Warren won the bet, as the S&P 500 returned 125.8 percent, trouncing the hedge funds' return of 36 percent. He donated the $2 million to Girls Incorporated of Omaha.

The chosen start date of January 1, 2008 was the beginning of one of the worst stock market years on record: –38 percent. The hedge funds performed better right off the start, but just like a cork that always wants to find its way to the surface, the S&P 500 outstripped the hedge funds by year four and provided almost four times the return by the end of the 10-year time period.

Warren Buffett knew his bet was a winner before the start. The history of hedge funds, and especially funds of funds (like Protégé), is so spotty that the odds were surely stacked in Warren's favor. Yes, hedge funds are sexy because of the periodic eye-popping returns in a hedge fund or two, but the math is generally pretty bad for the entire asset class unless, of course, you're a hedge fund manager. A study[34] published in June 2020 offers a composite view of the entire hedge fund universe from 1995 through 2016. This study was the work of Itzhak Ben-David and Justin Birru, both of Ohio State University, along with Andrea Rossi from the University of Arizona. The study offers insight into the way fees get allocated to investor accounts and how inconsistent high returns accelerate fees, but those fees are never given back in periods of low and negative returns. This causes fees to accrue at greater than the presumed underlying fee rate. The study included every registered and operating fund during the time window from 1995 to 2016. Although the stock market (S&P 500) returned 9.55 percent annually on average in this same time period, the average of all funds produced returns of just 5.4 percent before all fees. But it gets worse for the

---

34 Itzhak Ben-David, Justin Birru, and Andrea Rossi, "The Performance of Hedge Fund Performance Fees," Fisher College of Business Working Paper No. 2020-03-014, Charles A. Dice Working Paper No. 2020-14, June 24, 2020, https://ssrn.com/abstract=3630723 or http://dx.doi.org/10.2139/ssrn.3630723.

hedge funds. Once the management fees and incentive fees were accounted for, the net composite annual investor return was reduced to just 1.96 percent. This means that most (63.7 percent, to be exact) of the increase in value accrued to management fees and not investor returns. The math gets even worse when you realize that the hedge funds likely generated taxes in excess of those generated by the S&P 500 in the same period!

Let's take a deeper look at indexing by way of another analogy. My middle son, Stephen, is a sports statistics guru. He's always told me that baseball comes down to a few important statistics, none more important than batting average. Let's say you're a coach with a perennially struggling team. You need hitters. You meet a kid who wants to play on your team, but he tells you a strange fact: he only bunts. You're not particularly interested until he tells you these two mind-blowing morsels: he bats .900 and his technique can be learned perfectly by all your other team members. Not only will he get on base 90 percent of the time, but so will everyone else in the lineup! Swinging hard does make for exciting baseball and heroism by the likes of Babe Ruth. Hitting home runs will pack the stands. Yet a 90 percent on-base percentage while bunting would win every game.

So it is with indexing. It's a clear advantage until everyone else starts bunting, too. But as I said, that's unlikely and a long way off.

Yes, indexing is the cheapest and most efficient way to make money in the stock market, but that doesn't mean individual securities are a bad idea. They're not. In fact, the only way to outstrip the market and achieve excess returns over your lifetime is to invest in individual securities as a contrarian would. The average investor strategizes based on current "knowns." The problem is that everyone else already "knows the knowns," so they're reflected in current price. Let's say Tesla announces that their earnings for the next quarter are expected to grow by 5 percent compared to last year. That might seem like a good indicator that the stock price will rise in the future. But in reality, the minute those results are announced, the future earnings are priced into the shares. Your "opportunity" is gone. This is the "market efficiency" we've already discussed. A better strategy for gaining advantage would be achieved by asking, "How is what's known today going to affect tomorrow?" or "What mistakes are others making in their assessments today?"

Howard Marks refers to this contrarianism in his book *The Most Important Thing*: "First-level thinking says, 'It's a good company; let's buy the stock.' Second-level thinking says, 'It's a good company, but everyone thinks it's a great company, and it's not. So, the stock's overrated and overpriced; let's sell.' First-level thinking is simplistic and superficial, and just about everyone can do it (a bad sign for anything involving an attempt at superiority). All the first-level thinker needs is an opinion about the future, as in 'The outlook for the company is favorable, meaning the stock will go up.'"[35]

Ever played a game of chess? Chess requires each player to think ahead, closely watching their opponent's moves to anticipate what might come next. Each move causes a good chess player to ask, "How does that move change the dynamic of all the other pieces? Where are my opportunities? Where am I in jeopardy?" That's what makes chess a second-level-thinking game. People who are good at chess can think two or three, or even five, steps ahead before they make each move. This enables them to take into account the future outcomes that present decisions might bring about. Their next move may look counterintuitive, or contrarian in nature, but in reality, they're just thinking deeper than the average Joe.

How does this apply to investment methodology? Contrarians buy when there's blood in the streets and everyone is running for the hills. Sure, contrarians pause to ensure the company is fundamentally and financially sound (remember, investing is based on facts, not ideas), using metrics like profit margin and debt-to-equity ratio to quickly determine what a company is made of.

35 Howard Marks, *The Most Important Thing: Uncommon Sense for Thoughtful Investors* (New York: Columbia University Press, 2011).

Let's take a look at Target's data breach fiasco back in 2013. A cyberattack affected 41 million customers' payment information. When the news got out, their stock price plummeted by 20 percent as many of their stockholders bailed. Like any good contrarian and second-level thinker, I thought, *Target enjoys unmatched brand loyalty and sells household staples in hundreds of stores across the country. This PR scandal will be costly, but based on Target's proven strength, I bet there will be a steady comeback.* So I bought a 2.5 percent position in our Dividend Strategy and let it ride for years, collecting dividends as the price recovered and surpassed its pre-scandal price.

This is not an example of an expert investor achieving prodigious returns through above-average intellect and in-depth knowledge of company financials. Rather, it's an example of the nebulous second layer of thinking that the typical investor rarely gets to. Asking the question, "How will the outcomes from this decision bring about another layer of consequences?" doesn't come naturally to most. But you have to ask it to achieve superiority in tactical decision making.

There are a couple of ways to apply this thinking to your portfolio. To start, be contrarian when you buy the index. Buying more of an index when the future is particularly uncertain, such as during periods of wild downward market swings, is extremely emotionally difficult but can yield incredible returns. People often want to wait until they have enough confirming evidence piled up that it finally prompts them to act. The waiting, however, causes them to miss the bus.

Second, contrarian thinking is required when you attempt concentration, which you can best achieve using the two-portfolio theory, carving out a portion of your investable assets with which you're comfortable taking a greater risk (be mindful that most people don't do this well because they often put too much at risk). Making bets on individual companies when other investors are fleeing requires a stomach of steel, and the risk is often met with proportional returns.

CHOOSE WISELY

Take a look at the following graphic that shows how the Callan Periodic Table of Investment Returns[36] analyzes the returns of segments of the market year over year. It's not so important which segment did what. The important takeaway here is that a subsector that performs really poorly in one year can suddenly rise to the top of the heap in the following year. Seeing how often the very good years cozy up to the very bad years proves that whenever people only do what they should have already done, they will always be late to the profit party. The best gains in a

---

36 See appendix for full table or visit www.callan.com/periodic-table.

subsector of the marketplace happen long before anyone notices the transition. Choosing off the bottom of the "menu" could offer sweet rewards because, after periods of under-performance, these buys could position you early for the changing of the trend. Most investors make their choices by seeking company with those who look at the top of the "menu" for popular choices, which are not necessarily the wisest ones simply based on past price movement.

Truncated Version of the Callan Periodic Table

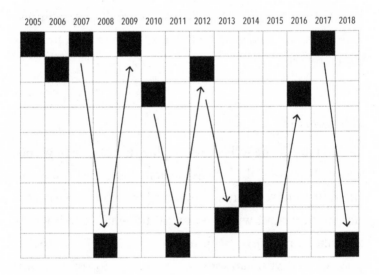

Emerging Markets

We've highlighted the Emerging Markets sector to show the tendency of sectors to perform very badly in one year before performing very well in the next. Other sectors have been removed to minimize confusion. To view Callan's Periodic Table of Investment Returns, go to www.callan.com/periodic-table.

So, yes, while the best way to make money in the stock market is with passive choices like indexing, excess returns come almost exclusively to those who act with a contrarian bias. Remember, this advantage is truly found by choosing off the bottom of the menu, especially after an extended string of trailing performance. Imagine the sellers at this point, who are surely not acting on a contrarian bias, rather likely just capitulating to their fear. But the slot machine with the highest odds of a payoff is the one with the most prolonged dry spell, and the same thing applies here. First-level thinking and conventional wisdom are manifested by those choosing off the top of the menu; that is the very picture of performance chasing (and likely not much catching).

Even so, this should only be done with great finesse because it is, in fact, risky. You may have a high-risk appetite, but that doesn't make you Superman. It's like Alex Honnold, a world-renowned free-climber, whose amygdala (the part of our brains responsible for generating emotions) has been the subject of many studies to determine the cause of his apparent lack of fear. Who else would be willing to scale Yosemite's El Capitan without ropes? He may have the guts and the skills required to be the first man to ever do it, but it doesn't mean he couldn't fall.

SO WHAT DO I DO?

I'm confident I've left you with a handful of necessary questions but none more pressing than *So what do I do?* Let's assume that you've suddenly realized that your managed account with your buddy at Merrill Lynch has lagged for many years and you're ready to make a change. Maybe you've also concluded that you have an honest understanding of your disposition toward your money, are truly okay with market risk, and simply want a more efficient outcome. I've got a few suggestions for you, the same suggestions I offer my friends and family:

- To start, stop the bleeding. Call off the active management of your account but don't liquidate.
- Determine your optimal stock-bond mix—for example, 70 percent stock, 30 percent bond and cash. This may be where you decide you want a fiduciary advisor along for the journey. Find one or contact me. My email address is gil.baumgarten@segmentwm.com.
- Sell your losers and your small gainers.
- Decide whether you will hold on to your large unrealized gain positions or if you will give them away to charity.
- Identify and purchase cheap, broad-market ETFs. I suggest SPY, VOO, and VTI.
- Consider a large allocation to Warren Buffett's Berkshire Hathaway (BRKB). I would suggest limiting this position to 10 percent of your total assets.

- Buy individual bonds from a reputable broker and arrange them in a ladder or sequence (if you want a lower risk allocation).
- And lastly, fix yourself an old-fashioned, relax, and make a toast to your brighter future.

And yes, it really is that simple. Cheers!

CONCLUSION

GONE FISHING

My goal in writing this book was not to treat every reader as a prospect for my business. Even though I'd be happy to field your phone calls, I wanted to write this book simply to pass along my experiences, knowledge, and as many nudges in the right direction as I could squeeze in while my daughter Allie had the time and space to work on this project with me. There's a lot more I could say, trust me. Yet, what I've said here aims to do one thing: help you.

Whether you put this book down and decide to call your broker or advisor, or you simply sit there and think to yourself, I hope you are now able to ask good questions and find sufficient answers. I recommend you take a minute to revisit your experiences with brokerage firms and how their services fit with your needs and expectations, inspect your biases and how they've impacted your investments, and assess your goals and objectives going forward and how you plan to stay the course.

As you set out, I want to arm you with some questions that will clarify your path forward.

QUESTIONS TO ASK YOURSELF

What do I want? Do I recognize my emotional biases? Do I seek results or just emotional fulfillment? Am I willing to do hard things? What's my risk appetite these days? Should I hire an advisor? If so, what type? If I hire an advisor, will I let *them* do hard things? If I already have a broker, do I understand where his allegiances lie and what that means for our relationship?

QUESTIONS FOR YOUR ADVISOR

Are you a fiduciary? Do you earn commissions of any kind? What about 12b-1 fees? Do you manage for after-tax return? Do you believe in low-cost investing? Do you consider yourself a contrarian? Do you believe in tactically managing risk? What about creating portfolios for the long haul? What impediments does your firm put in the way of you advocating for my success?

As I see it, you may find yourself somewhere on the spectrum of investor preparedness after answering these and similar questions. Your knowledge of how the markets work and the advice you have assembled can make a world of difference as you set out with a fresh mindset. You don't want to find yourself with no idea how the markets work and no one guiding you. You'd be in a slightly better position with some idea of what's going on with your money and a broker who isn't really looking out for you but offers some advice. The next step up would mean getting a pretty good idea of what's going on with your money, and a broker who *is* looking out for you. The pinnacle of the awareness/readiness spectrum is an investor who has money, understands how the market and taxes work, and has a fiduciary advisor who *must* look out for him.

THE VALUE OF HAVING A GUIDE

I'm a big fan of hunting and fishing. So much so, I go on a big trip at least twice a year. Sometimes I go with my wife, and sometimes I take one or more of my kids somewhere we've never been before. More often, I go with a group of clients and buddies. We go back to our favorite spots, time and again. I used to go on these trips ready and willing to fend for myself because it seemed easy enough and I figured it would be much more rewarding and a lot less expensive. It didn't take long for me to realize that I was remarkably wrong. One of my trips went so wrong that I wound up publishing an article in *Field and Stream* titled "The Elk Hunt from Hell." We suffered flat tires, ran out of fuel, lost our Jeep keys, found our Jeep keys, high centered the Jeep on a boulder and damaged the transmission, and spent an hour looking for the missing remote control for the winch, all in the rain. And that's only a fraction of all that went south.

There's an insightful old saying that goes, "If you think hiring a professional is expensive, try hiring an amateur." This is why I mentioned having a fishing guide in Chapter 7. I now know that if I took on all the responsibility myself, I would have to piece together lodging, boat rentals, fuel, food preparation, rugged portage navigation, and in the end, spend an inordinate amount of time and money getting the right gear with us at just the right time. And so, I hung up those cleats.

I love hiring a guide and having them plan it all out for us. Why? It's worth it. Not just because of the prep work. Guides spend years receiving groups just like ours. They know how to give us the best experience possible. What does that look like? Practicing their trade. Having the right gear. Observing patterns in the wild. Learning about every species in the water. Knowing the climate and smells and sounds. Planning for the fact that the tides can rise and fall 30 feet daily. Trying out different methods and tricks for catching certain fish at certain times of day. They know where to be and when so that we can have the best chance of making our dreams come true. They know that certain fish have patterns of behavior that they repeat year after year, especially migrating salmon. How is a neophyte to know all that? Sure, the guides have also experienced many failures, too, but those failures can help us avoid the same mistakes.

You know what the guide will never do, though? Guarantee a trophy fish. Why? They can't predict what's going to bite. They only know what might give you the best shot at it. That's what we really want from them: to advocate for our success. We want them to know what they're doing, to watch out for us, to offer their expert advice, to use their experience and their equipment to our benefit. I also want to know that I'm not endangering myself in ways I cannot predict. Add in the fact that their services also mean the clean sheets and the warm campfire back at the lodge are not my responsibility to provide. You bet I'm willing to pay a premium price for all of that.

Honestly, it's a lot like the money management business. There are folks like me out there who spend their time practicing their trade, learning the terrain, observing patterns, testing methodologies, and developing best practices, all so clients can have the best shot at doing well with their money.

Although I spent some time herein castigating the brokerage business, I will say once again that conflicted advice is still generally better than no advice at all. Sometimes conflicted advice is perfectly sufficient. Still, hopefully, you are better equipped now to discern whether you should expect your advisor to do what's in your best interest or whether you need to apply a more critical eye to his suggestions.

If I've done what I set out to do in writing this book, you will understand how to piece these things together. I hope you will go out and find the right guide for your situation and do so with full knowledge of what you're up against, a more complete understanding of your biases regarding your money, and a few tools to tame your own demons. It is my sincere hope that you can now better muster the resources to go out and invest your money without being FOOLISH.

ACKNOWLEDGMENTS

I want to thank all the people who helped me write this book whether they know it or not. Some were directly involved, like my daughter, Allie B. Dupree, who worked painstakingly for 18 months to help me assemble my scattered thoughts. Her partner in that crime was Jennifer Heerensperger, who has been my right hand at work for the past nine years and has made my job and my life better accordingly. Allie and her brothers, my two sons, Brian and Stephen, have provided endless inspiration for me and plenty of opportunities to teach them an economics lesson or three. It's all about incentives. I made sure they felt the pain of their occasional poor choices, and I am confident they would admit they are better for it.

I want to thank my longtime friend and hunting partner Jim Fearnow, who hired me as a broker trainee in his

EF Hutton branch office in 1984. Jim believed in me and taught me a great deal about doing the brokerage business honorably, and for that, I'm truly grateful.

One of my heroes, Jack Bogle, dedicated his life to the betterment of the individual investor. I wrote him a letter that I have framed in my office along with his handwritten response in 2018, the year before his death. I told him that he had done more for my business and learning than anyone. I'm glad I took the opportunity to thank him then. His work to expose the ways Wall Street siphons off client money for itself by providing often futile services gave rise to alternate paths. Those paths eventually evolved into the ETF business of which I have been an advocate and early adopter, leading to much of my success. Jack's work on indexing is applicable to other areas of portfolio construction, my knowledge of which has led to countless other opportunities in my business. I told Jack that I agreed with Warren Buffett, who said that Jack Bogle had done more for the American investor than any other individual. I also encouraged Jack to reconsider his opposition to ETFs since their positives outweigh their negatives. He gave me a humble aw-shucks response and acknowledged he had come around to my way of thinking on ETFs and intended to correct his prior opinions on ETFs in his last book, *Stay the Course: The Story of Vanguard and the Index Revolution.*

No list of thank-yous would be complete without mentioning Mom. My mother, Gwyn Baumgarten, has been a lifelong cheerleader of mine and taught me a great deal about standing up for what I believe is right. I learned my muckraking skills from her!

And finally, to my wife, Sue, who understands me and encourages me to be the best man I can be. She listens to me and knows I can always aim higher and can accomplish almost anything I set my mind to. She too has been a cheerleader for me and challenges me in all the right ways. I am grateful to God for her and for His provision in my life in so many ways.

APPENDIX

Representation of the Callan Periodic Table of Investment Returns

Annual Returns for Key Indices in Order of Performance (2000–2019)

	2000	2001	2002	2003	2004	2005	2006	2007	2008	2009	2010	2011	2012	2013	2014	2015	2016	2017	2018	2019
1	13.84%	8.43%	22.37%	55.82%	37.96%	34.00%	41.12%	39.38%	5.24%	78.51%	26.85%	7.84%	27.73%	38.82%	15.02%	1.38%	21.31%	37.28%	1.87%	31.49%
2	13.84%	5.28%	10.26%	47.25%	25.55%	15.35%	32.17%	12.44%	4.39%	58.21%	41.12%	4.98%	18.23%	32.39%	13.69%	0.55%	17.13%	24.21%	0.01%	25.52%
3	6.18%	4.42%	2.82%	40.69%	20.38%	14.47%	25.71%	11.03%	2.06%	37.13%	18.88%	4.36%	16.41%	21.02%	5.97%	0.05%	11.96%	21.83%	-2.08%	22.49%
4	-3.02%	2.49%	1.78%	39.42%	18.33%	4.91%	18.37%	6.97%	-26.16%	33.67%	15.12%	2.11%	16.35%	7.44%	4.89%	-0.79%	11.19%	14.65%	-2.15%	21.91%
5	-3.91%	-3.91%	-1.37%	28.97%	12.54%	4.55%	15.79%	5.49%	-33.79%	27.17%	15.06%	0.10%	16.00%	3.67%	2.45%	-3.04%	4.06%	10.51%	-4.38%	18.44%
6	-5.86%	-3.75%	-6.16%	28.68%	11.13%	3.07%	11.85%	5.00%	-37.00%	26.47%	8.95%	-4.18%	15.81%	0.07%	0.03%	-4.41%	2.75%	10.36%	-5.63%	14.32%
7	-9.11%	-3.81%	-15.80%	19.36%	10.88%	2.74%	8.16%	1.87%	-43.56%	7.53%	6.54%	-6.46%	4.21%	-2.02%	-2.19%	-4.47%	2.65%	7.50%	-11.01%	8.72%
8		-11.89%	-20.48%	4.10%	4.34%	2.43%	4.85%	1.57%	-48.21%	5.93%	4.95%	-12.21%	4.09%	-2.60%	-3.09%	-6.02%	1.49%	3.54%	-14.09%	5.09%
9	-13.37%	-21.40%	-22.10%	1.15%	1.33%	-8.65%	4.33%	-7.39%	-53.33%	0.21%	0.13%	-18.42%	0.11%	-3.08%	-4.32%	-14.92%	0.33%	0.86%	-14.57%	2.28%

Key:

- Emerging Markets
- Real Estate
- US Fixed Income
- Global ex-US Fixed Income
- Developed ex-US Equity
- High Yield
- Cash Equivalent
- Large-Cap Equity
- Small-Cap Equity

GLOSSARY

12b-1—The servicing fee hidden within mutual fund expenses that is returned to the brokerage firm that holds the security in a customer's account. Derided by many as a kickback, the fee is intended to provide compensation as an incentive to a broker to handle client questions or service issues.

Account—An account held at a brokerage firm or bank that has separate accounting and reporting by that account number, allowing brokerage firms to segregate their fiduciary and nonfiduciary business and follow regulatory rules on where they have conflicts of interest and how they must disclose these to clients.

Advisory Firm—This is most often a fiduciary and fee-only firm but could be a firm dually registered with the

Financial Industry Regulatory Authority for commission activity and the Securities and Exchange Commission for advisory fee business.

Alpha—The holy grail of investing that is seldom experienced but pursued with great fervor. The core of active security selection is the pursuit of alpha or value added in the form of lower risk for a given return level or a higher return for a given risk level.

Annuity—A tax-deferred product that can mix fixed accounts with mutual funds and/or provide a fixed monthly payout.

Asset Manager—Most often an independent manager hired for stock picking or bond selection. Asset managers are often employed as subadvisors on brokerage platforms and offer little to no personalized investor services.

Back-End Load—Annuities and certain share classes of open-end mutual funds (mostly B and C) often have a contingent deferred sales charge (CDSC). The CDSC is a penalty levied against investors who liquidate before they reach a predefined holding period in order to recover commissions paid up front to a broker while subjecting the fund assets to increased management fees as an alternate method of recovery for the fund.

Beta—A measure of a stock's or portfolio's volatility as compared to the market. A beta score of 1 means complete correlation. Beta describes the activity of a security's returns as it responds to swings in the market.

Bid-Ask Spread—The bid-ask spread refers to the differential in price between the highest price a buyer will pay and the lowest price a seller will accept. Most investments such as stocks or bonds have one price if you're buying and another if you're selling. Many middlemen make their living in that spread of coming and going and often will have their own money at risk.

Bogle, John "Jack" C.—Jack Bogle was the founder and chief executive of The Vanguard Group and is credited with creating the first index fund.

Bond—A tradeable loan with fixed and measurable terms.

Broker—A professional trader who buys and sells financial instruments on behalf of clients. In order to maintain their Series 7 license (which gives them legal authority to sell securities and receive commissions on trades), brokers must be registered with the Financial Industry Regulatory Authority and must be employed by a brokerage firm. The employing firm regulates the broker's activity, what he or she is allowed to present to clients, and who gets paid on commissions or fee-sharing arrangements. Brokers cannot be fiduciaries but can offer fiduciary services provided by others, such as an advisory firm's separately managed account services, also known as a wrap account.

Brokerage Firm—A Financial Industry Regulatory Authority-regulated firm that facilitates the buying and selling of financial instruments for a commission, shared fees, or soft dollars and is allowed wide latitude for conflicts of interest with clients.

Buffett, Warren—A legendary investor and multibillionaire who is chairman of Berkshire Hathaway.

Capital Gain or Loss—The change in market value above or below original purchase price.

Call Option—A call option is a financial instrument that gives the buyer an option to buy an asset (e.g., stocks) at an agreed-upon price on or before a particular date.

Churning—An illegal practice where a broker makes trades in a customer's account merely to derive a commission.

Closed-End Fund—A mutual fund with a fixed number of shares that does not offer purchase or redemption liquidity. Liquidity is provided by the listed marketplace. An exchange-traded fund (ETF) is a kind of closed-end fund, but an ETF doesn't have a fixed number of shares.

Commission—A charge added to purchases or subtracted from sales representing compensation to a broker or brokerage firm.

Commodity—Often a bit of a misnomer since the term is used as a substitute for the futures market when discussing the underlying true commodity, such as bacon, orange juice, or interest rates.

Correlation—A statistical measurement of the similarity of two data sets.

Cost Basis—The investor's cost to purchase a security by which the gain or loss will be measured against for future taxation.

Coupon—This is the percentage rate agreed to in an original bond offering and is agreed to be paid by the borrower. The term *coupon* is often referenced in dollar terms as well as in "I received my $500 coupon payment."

Custodian—The firm providing custody services.

Custody—The brokerage service provided for safekeeping of customer cash and securities.

DALBAR—An investment research organization similar to Morningstar. DALBAR focuses on what investors do when buying funds, whereas Morningstar focuses only on the funds themselves.

Discretion—The handing-off of trading decisions to a third party and the acceptance of those trades by an investor in his own account. Brokers are not allowed to have discretion in an account for which they earn commission (fee-only accounts can allow brokers to have discretion).

Dividend—Cashflow distributed by qualified corporations to shareholders, which receives preferential tax treatment similar to long-term gains.

Donor-Advised Fund—A fund that receives charitable contributions of donors and holds and invests them until the donor indicates the final designated charity.

Dow 30—A long-standing index comprised of 30 large companies whose stocks are representative of the market as a whole.

Dual Registration—In the brokerage business, licenses have everything to do with how an advisor is being compensated. Commission business is always governed by the Financial Industry Regulatory Authority and fee-based advisory is always governed by the Securities and Exchange Commission. Some firms get paid from both lines of business and must be dually registered.

Enron—This company experienced a spectacular corporate flameout in the late '90s involving energy, leverage, hubris, and creative accounting.

Equity—A listed share of a company representing a shared interest in company ownership. Each share is a small slice of the company. The terms *stock* and *equity* are interchangeable.

Error Account—A slush fund that all brokerages maintain and use to reconcile erroneous trades or square up inefficient outcomes.

Exchange-Traded Fund (ETF)—A variation of a closed-end fund, listed on an exchange for trading liquidity. ETFs do not have shared accounting with other holders.

Fiduciary Advisor—One who is legally bound to limit or vanquish conflicts of interest in advising and dealing with clients and their investments and who cannot earn a commission on trades. A fiduciary advisor is paid for their advice, not for executing trades. In theory, this separation encourages the fiduciary advisor to always give the best financial advice to their clients whether that advice encourages a trade. (Meanwhile, a broker is incentivized to execute trades because that is how they receive commission.) Fiduciary advisors must be registered with the Securities and Exchange Commission as a registered investment advisor (RIA).

Financial Advisor—Any financial service provider who can legally give financial advice. Stockbrokers, fiduciary advisors, and many others are all known professionally as financial advisors or simply "advisors," even though their individual roles vary greatly. This naming often confuses the general public.

Financial Ecosystem—The totality of stock and bond markets, along with related mutual funds, banking, mortgages, brokerages, and advisory businesses.

Financial Industry Regulatory Authority (FINRA)— Formerly called the NASD, it's the self-regulatory body of brokerages who establish their own rules of customer interactions under the supervision of the Securities and Exchange Commission.

Form CRS—The Client Relationship Summary Form is limited to two pages and must address each brokerage firm's conflicts of interest and how they are mitigated. It must be presented to clients at account inception and annually thereafter.

Front-End Load—The mutual fund structure that pays commissions to brokers under Financial Industry Regulatory Authority regulations whereby principal is withdrawn up front from fund purchasers and returned to brokerage dealers as a sales commission.

Front Running—This is an illegal practice whereby advance knowledge of client trades can create an exploitable opportunity to trade against the client. It is not illegal if the firm or broker merely sells the info to a third party, provided that the front running that occurs from such information operates within the existing bid-ask spread. Running the stock up or down in front of a buy or sell order and the broker using their position for gain are the two objectionable results.

Futures—Similar to options, futures are contracts priced to reflect the risks of forced delivery of a finite good at a definite time at a definite location.

Glass-Steagall Act—A regulatory act passed in the 1930s that regulated certain separations of the financial services businesses such as brokerage and insurance.

Gramm-Leach-Bliley Act—The 1998 act that repealed Glass-Steagall and replaced it with a looser regulatory framework. This is often cited as laying the framework for the 2008 financial crisis.

Hedge Fund—Originally designed as a noncorrelating hedge to stock exposure (i.e., long/short), the category now includes the trading of all liquid stocks, bonds, and options and often employs leverage and algorithms. The funds usually have restricted liquidity.

Heuristics—A natural human tendency toward snap judgment using comparative relationships.

Household—The aggregation of all accounts owned by an investor or couple regardless of style or number of accounts, including IRAs, single, joint name, and so forth.

Indexing—The deliberate allocation of securities in an investment with the intent of matching the underlying comparative benchmark. This can lead to low fees and low tax drag.

Interest—The payment that provides commensurate compensation for the time and risks taken on a loan, quoted as an annual rate.

Investment Manager/Money Manager—An advisor for hire who makes investment decisions for investors through mutual funds or separately managed account services, which are based on a particular strategy and are not customized for each individual investor. These managers may work as a part of a brokerage firm or be independent and are usually registered with the Securities and Exchange Commission as a registered investment advisor. These managers almost never collect a commission for their services but instead charge a fee calculated as a percentage of assets under management.

IRA—An individual retirement account that allows tax-deferred savings until age 72 when forced taxable distributions begin.

Listed Security—A security that trades on an exchange such as the NASDAQ or New York Stock Exchange after a company has undergone an initial public offering.

Long-Term Capital—A hedge fund that experienced a spectacular flameout similar to that of the UBS YES program. In 1998, Long Term Capital blew up tens of billions in a seemingly low-risk leveraged bond trade. When interest rates hiccupped, the bond trade imploded and the ensuing ripple effects caused a mini financial crisis.

Managed Account—An account service provided by brokerage firms where trading commissions and separate manager fees are waived for the sake of an all-encompassing fee that pays the brokerage firm, the broker, and the manager in a split arrangement. Also known as a wrap account or separately managed account.

Markup—When a firm takes possession of an investment from a seller, client, or other brokerage with their own capital where they increase the buyer's price or decrease the seller's price to earn a "spread." This is regulated as a commission.

Modern Portfolio Theory (MPT)—A theory that combines the theoretical work of William Sharpe and Harry Markowitz. In 1990, they won the Nobel Prize in Economics for work they published in the 1960s. MPT essentially says that security selection doesn't matter for a number of reasons and asset allocation drives results.

Municipal Bond (Muni)—A tradeable loan to a local municipality such as a state or school district. Interest earned is tax-free to investors.

Mutual Fund—An investment vehicle that allows commingled investment with mitigated counterparty risks since the pool is regulated. A mutual fund could be invested in stocks or bonds depending on the mandate expressed in the prospectus.

Occam's Razor—A philosophical theory that surmises that the simplest solution to a problem is usually the best one. Named after a fourteenth-century friar named William of Occam.

Open-End Fund—A mutual fund with an open structure that allows daily entrance and exit of new purchases and redemptions. Open-end funds have shared accounting with other shareholders.

Option—A financial instrument that gives the buyer an

option to buy or sell an asset (like stocks) at an agreed-upon price on or before a particular date.

Option Premium—The cash value derived from selling or buying an option.

Pay Grid—The spreadsheet that sorts out the broker's cut.

Prospectus—The offering and disclosure document of a mutual fund. Distribution of a fund's prospectus to investors is required at purchase and annually thereafter.

Protégé Partners—A fund-of-funds manager who allocates client dollars into an array of other hedge funds. This group took the other side of the million-dollar bet offered by Warren Buffett that a simple stock index fund would outrun the smartest guys in the room over the decade from 2008 to 2018. Warren won the bet handily and gave the $2 million to charity.

Put Option—A put option is a financial instrument that gives the buyer an option to sell an asset (e.g., stocks) at an agreed-upon price on or before a particular date.

Realized Gain—The difference in the value for which a security was *sold* and its purchase price. A realized gain can be either long term (held for at least 366 days) or short term (held for less than 366 days). Long-term gains have a tax cap lower than the marginal rate of the investor; most often, it's about half the marginal tax rate but capped currently at 23.8 percent. Short-term gains generate the most egregious tax outcome because the highest marginal rate of the investor applies.

Realized Loss—The difference in the value of a security that was sold for less than the purchase price. Realized losses can offset realized gains for tax purposes.

Regulation Best Interest (Reg BI)—The watered-down legislation adopted in 2020 that sets forth new rules of engagement between brokers and customers. Best interest in name only, the rules still allow conflicts to exist albeit with simpler disclosure in Form CRS.

Roth IRA—A tax-free retirement account that is restricted to only lower-compensated rungs of the economic ladder. Off limits to high-net-worth investors unless they are converting regular IRAs to Roth.

S&P 500—A broad market index of 500 stocks that represent the marketplace for US-listed stocks.

Sales Load—Some mutual funds carve off a percentage of a client's purchases or redemptions, which are returned to the custodian brokerage as a finder's fee or commission.

Securities and Exchange Commission (SEC)—The governing body responsible for regulating the securities industry and the Financial Industry Regulatory Authority.

Security—The broad term used to encompass financial instruments such as stocks, bonds, options, mutual funds, money funds, and so forth.

Share Class—Mutual funds' subclasses, which differentiate the underlying fees charged, often determined within the latitude of a broker's recommendation but may be otherwise required based on purchase amount.

SPIVA Report—Standard & Poor's maintains index composition and provides data on weighted measurements, which they rent and license to the advisory community. They also publish the *SPIVA Report*, which tracks active managers and measurements of their competitive returns against a relative benchmark.

Spot—The institutional live price in the marketplace at a moment in time for any commodity or currency that reflects large size and liquidity, void of all commissions or markups.

Spread—A form of commission in which a firm purchases a security with its own money and resells the security to a customer at a markup.

Step-Up in Basis—The tax law providing relief from capital gains taxes at death, which erases prior purchase history for tax purposes and replaces it with the value at the date of death. This rule does not apply to annuities or retirement accounts.

Sticky—Complicated enough to encourage people to leave things as they are.

Stock—A shared interest in company ownership. Each share of stock is a small slice of the company. A company's stock can be listed on a stock exchange and traded in the open market, or unlisted, in which case ownership of the company is traded privately.

Suitability—The standard of care for brokerage firms interacting with customers. Recommendations can be conflicted and self-serving as long as the customer's underlying needs are met.

Tax Drag—The reduction of potential return by way of taxation.

Tax Loss Carryforward—Losses on sales of securities are only deductible against ordinary income to a $3,000 annual maximum. However, losses above that amount can be carried forward to future years and used to offset gains on sales until consumed.

The Market—Collectively, the stock market is an auction place for listed stocks comprised of many markets but mostly the New York Stock Exchange (NYSE) and National Association of Securities Dealers Automated Quotations (NASDAQ).

Two-Portfolio Theory—This is a Segment Wealth moniker for the process of physically separating a portfolio into high-risk and low-risk components. This has both financial and psychological benefits to investors.

UBS YES Program—An add-on feature offered to UBS clients who could use the borrowing potential of their accounts in a seemingly low-risk leveraged bond spread trading program. The strategy collapsed and imploded over a billion dollars for clients, and UBS was forced to settle legal claims.

Unrealized Gain—The retained and unsold increase from purchase price of an asset.

Unrealized Loss—The retained and unsold decrease from purchase price of an asset.

Wealth Manager—One who makes customized recommendations for individuals based on risk tolerance, tax status, and liquidity requirements. May be a broker but usually a fee-only fiduciary registered as a registered investment advisor.

Wrap Account—A brokerage service that combines the compensation of three providers in one cost, hence "wrapped": brokerage, advice/service, and security selection. Often presented in the pursuit of alpha.

ABOUT THE AUTHOR

GIL BAUMGARTEN, one of the nation's top financial advisors, is the Founder and President of Segment Wealth Management, an RIA financial advisory firm based in Houston, Texas, with over a billion dollars in client assets under advisement. Gil began his career in the securities and investment industry in the 1980s, working for some of the most renowned brokerage firms on Wall Street including EF Hutton, UBS, and Smith Barney (what is today Morgan Stanley). However, Gil found Wall Street routinely prioritized its own interests over those of clients. In 2010, Gil jumped off the brokerage train to found Segment, a fee-only fiduciary firm that is legally required to hold its clients' interests above the firm's. This kind of allegiance to clients creates relationships based not just on advice but also on advocacy, which is why Gil trademarked the phrase, "More than Advice...Advocacy." Every action taken by Gil and his team at Segment finds its center in this core philosophy.

Part psychologist, part artist, part financial advisor, and bona fide math whiz, Gil carefully constructs efficient portfolios using a multidimensional approach to radically minimize performance drag from taxes and fees. This approach brings asset management in-house, forgoing fee-heavy open-end mutual funds and separately managed accounts, and instead trading in a tax-sensitive way to produce results that reliably outperform traditional brokerage firm methodologies.

Named one of the Top 20 Exchange-Traded Fund Thought Leaders in America by *Barron's* and *The Wall Street Journal*, Gil's expertise is frequently recognized and called upon. He is a nine-time recipient of the *Barron's* Top 1,200 Financial Advisors distinction, has been ranked by *Barron's* as one of the 50 Best Advisors in Texas and by the *Financial Times* as one of the Top 300 Registered Investment Advisors in America, and is a perennial recipient of the *Texas Monthly* magazine Five-Star Advisor Award based on an independent study of client satisfaction. Having participated as one of six beta testers in a national UBS program of all-ETF portfolios, Gil is one of only a handful of professional money managers with a 17-year track record running 100 percent ETF portfolios. Beyond that, Gil has been a guest commentator on Bloomberg

Radio and even hosted his own radio talk show called *Dollars and Sense.*

An avid outdoorsman, Gil has traveled the world hunting and fishing. He excels at activities involving precision; he was his university's billiard champion and enjoys archery, darts, skeet, and marksmanship. Gil is an award-winning woodworker specializing in a particular art form called segmentation from which his firm gets its name. Segmentation is the assembly of various species of wood, cut to fit in a precise pattern. This knack for precision extends to Gil's investment strategies, where risk components and financial strategies are added and subtracted from client accounts with the same attention to detail.

Gil and his wife, Sue, love the city of Houston. They are both present and past board members and volunteers of numerous charities including Young Life, Young Lives, Coastal Conservation Association, LifeHouse, Star of Hope, Lamar High School Alumni Association Board, and the National Christian Foundation. They have three grown children, Brian, Stephen, and Allie, who, with their spouses, are each making their dad proud of how they live their lives.